Getting Started in
Public Speaking

Third Edition

James Payne
Diana Prentice Carlin

 **Glencoe**

New York, New York   Columbus, Ohio   Chicago, Illinois   Peoria, Illinois   Woodland Hills, California

ABOUT THE AUTHORS

James Payne has been a speech, debate, and English instructor for over 20 years. Currently he is an assistant principal at Blue Valley High School in Stilwell, Kansas. He has made numerous presentations on speech communication at state and national meetings and is co-author of *Public Speaking Today!*

Diana Prentice Carlin teaches in the Communication Studies Department at the University of Kansas at Lawrence. She also taught speech, debate, and English for eight years at the secondary level. Professor Carlin has co-authored textbooks on debate and group discussion, and is a co-author of *Public Speaking Today!*

Cover Photos:
Top and bottom left and right: Jeff Ellis, Jeff Ellis Photography
Middle left: Courtesy of North East Independent School District, San Antonio, Texas

Copyright © 1994, 1990, 1985 The McGraw-Hill Companies, Inc. All Rights reserved. Except as permitted under the United States Copyright Act of 1976, no part of this publication may be reproduced or distributed in any form or by any means, or stored in a database retrieval system, without prior written permission of the publisher.

Send all Inquiries to:
Glencoe/McGraw-Hill
8787 Orion Place
Columbus, OH 43240

ISBN : 0-8442-5597-1
Printed in the United States of America
11 12 13 14 <u>069</u> 08

No skill offers greater possibilities for reward than the skill of public speaking. Even a brief look at the leaders we admire and the jobs we desire reveals one thing: skilled presentation of personal viewpoints before large groups of people is a prerequisite to success.

Successful public speakers are made, not born. You can better your future by developing and refining your public speaking skills.

Although you may now see greater need for writing and social communication, you should also realize that the skills important to public speaking often improve writing, conversational speaking, group discussion, and social confidence.

This book is full of opportunities for you. Each lesson covers skills that can improve your public speaking.

Lesson 1 will acquaint you with the importance of public speaking in our society. It will give you a vocabulary for the study of speech. It may also relieve some of the tension you have about being in a speech class.

Lessons 2–5 will focus your attention on the audience. In these lessons you will learn how to select a good topic, analyze an audience, understand audience responses, and listen effectively.

Lessons 6–9 present strategies for preparing and presenting yourself as a speaker. In these lessons you will learn about types of speeches, nonverbal delivery, voice, and style. These lessons will enable you to make your message your own.

Lessons 10–14 help you construct an effective message. These lessons will examine research techniques, organizational patterns, effective introductions and conclusions, and the two major types of speeches.

To help you study public speaking, we have included several special features.

First, the "Picture This . . ." sections beginning each lesson ask you to respond to real public speaking problems. As students beginning to study speech, you can benefit from the experiences of others who have faced problem situations.

Second, each lesson offers several ways of learning about speech. In addition to a speech exercise for each lesson, you can also learn through group discussion activities and writing projects.

Third, this book offers three sample speeches to illustrate good message development. Examples of speech outlines, introductions, and conclusions further illustrate good public speaking techniques. The glossary at the end will make your study easier.

By bringing to this class your enthusiasm and desire to achieve, and by working with your teacher, you can improve your public speaking. This book gives you the materials and the insight you need.

CONTENTS

1

The Importance of
Public Speaking

Picture This...

Your school's graduation requirements are being reviewed. A large group of citizens has proposed adding two requirements. The group favors one more course in English composition and one more in mathematics. The group says these requirements would help prepare students for college and careers.

Three meetings will take place before a decision is made. First, approximately 100 students will meet to write a response to the proposal. Second, the teachers will hold a special faculty meeting. They will ask some students to speak. Third, a group of fifty citizens who are undecided will also meet. You have a strong opinion about the added requirements. You know that someone who disagrees with you will speak before you. What will you do?

A. Give a speech in favor of your position to the citizen group.
B. Give a speech in favor of your position at the faculty meeting.
C. Give a speech in favor of your position at the student meeting.
D. Express your opinions privately, but not give a speech.
E. Agree to debate the student who opposes your viewpoint.
F. Refuse to express an opinion in public.

INTRODUCTION: The Importance of Public Speaking

Frequently we make choices by answering two simple questions: "What good will this do me?" and "What will this cost me?" These two questions guide our decisions about which clothes we buy, how we vote, or what classes we take.

As a student learning about giving speeches, you are probably asking, "What good *will* this do me? I don't plan to be a politician or a teacher." Still, there are many times both in school and out of school when you will have the chance to speak in public.

ACTIVITY 1   In small groups of four to six, make a list of typical situations in which a person may be called on to speak in public. After you compile your list, select the "Top Ten" situations. Choose a spokesperson to share your list with the class.

When you ask, "What good will studying speech do me?" you are asking about opportunities and risks. Opportunities are situations that give you a chance to gain a favorable result. A good job offer is usually viewed as an opportunity. If you play a sport, a spot in the starting lineup would be an opportunity for you.

However, almost every opportunity involves *risk*. Accepting a good job offer requires you to risk something: moving from familiar surroundings; changing from an older, more secure job; reducing the time given to social life; or taking a chance that the job may not be permanent. "What will this cost me?" is a question about risk. A risk is a possibility of harm or loss. A thoughtful look at a situation usually reveals risks—some major, some minor. The old saying, "nothing ventured, nothing gained," shows the relationship between opportunities and risks. If nothing is ever risked, nothing can be gained. You will never know the benefits of a new job unless you take the risks of accepting it.

Every speaking situation presents a set of opportunities and risks. In most situations the opportunities are far greater than the risks. With practice, the risks become fewer and the opportunities become greater. Just as a baseball player practices every day in order to reduce the risk of errors, a public speaker learns and practices the fundamentals to reduce the risks. You will have many opportunities to practice your skills—in your education, your career, and as a citizen.

OPPORTUNITIES AT SCHOOL

You have been in school long enough to know that it provides many opportunities for students who are willing to speak in public. Students who will talk to others in reports, group discussions, and meetings can become the leaders and achievers in a school.

During the years ahead, your opportunities to speak to others will increase. You will be given the opportunity to improve your grades by making speeches. Your impact on school and community affairs will grow stronger as you learn to voice your opinions. In fact, some college classes are made up entirely of students' oral reports.

The opportunities for public speaking are very attractive. "Picture This. . ." at the beginning of the lesson shows that public speaking makes it possible for many to hear your opinions.

ACTIVITY 2 Think about the classes offered at your school, both required and elective. Identify and list at least five assignments given by teachers that require public speaking. For each assignment listed, write down the opportunities and the risks. (Note that receiving a grade is *not* an opportunity.)

OPPORTUNITIES ON THE JOB

When you train for a job, you learn skills that are in demand. Many people forget that public speaking is one of those skills, even though evidence of its importance is everywhere. Many large insurance agencies require *all* new employees (not only salespeople) to take a course in speech. Many banks insist that their employees take a speech class. It might surprise you that many factories require speech instruction for employees who want to advance to higher-paying jobs in management.

A major aircraft company, for example, invests in its own public speaking program for employees. Business and industry must see a high value in speech training to invest so much time and money. A speech is such a powerful tool that many business leaders hire speech writers. Recently, the president of a major corporation advertised for a speech writer at a yearly salary of $90,000!

The number of speaking opportunities in business and industry shows why speech training is so important. When a crew chief or supervisor meets with a ten-person crew, that is an opportunity for public speaking. A sales meeting, a banquet, and a staff meeting are opportunities for employees to improve their positions through public speaking.

ACTIVITY 3 Write a description of a job or career you want to have ten or fifteen years from now. Explain what opportunities for public speaking exist in that job or career. (If you are unsure, talk to someone who currently has that job.)

OPPORTUNITIES IN A DEMOCRACY

If you stop to think about it, there are more opportunities to speak in this country than in most others. The Constitution of the United States recognizes the importance of speech in a free society, and it protects your right and freedom to speak in the First Amendment. The founders of the country knew that people who are free to govern themselves must have the right to speak out.

Perhaps you do not believe that you have much to do with politics and social issues. Think about laws that affect you. Are you completely satisfied with all of them? Think about the rules of your school or the ordinances of your city. Can you suggest positive changes? These questions are political. Even if you do not run for a political office yourself, you have the opportunity to control your own future by speaking out about issues that concern you. School board and city council meetings offer built-in opportunities for the average citizen to speak out.

ACTIVITY 4 Examine your local newspaper. Locate five examples of meetings or activities that involved public speaking. Make a list of these situations and then write the opportunities that could result from each one.

Why Start Now?   If all the opportunities for public speaking are in your future, why should you worry about speech *now*? The answer to that can be found in any other course you might be taking. If you did not worry about learning to type until you had a secretarial job, you would probably never get the job. If you did not want to learn to swim until you got a job as a camp counselor, you would probably never be a camp counselor.

Stated simply, you cannot avoid the opportunity to speak in public. You may say ''no'' every time a speaking situation comes up, but by doing so, you lose all the benefits that can be gained: better grades, financial reward, respect, and control of your own future.

THE RISKS

You have explored some of the opportunities, but what about the risks? Risks may be hard to define, but they are definitely there.

A survey of adults revealed that people fear public speaking more than anything else. Those surveyed listed it over death, the dark, snakes, and heights. Why? Perhaps it is because they could avoid the other fears. If you fear snakes, you can avoid places where there are snakes. It is different with public speaking. It is impossible to go through school, a job, and life in a democracy without encountering speaking situations. Public speaking may be the number one fear because it is so necessary in our society, but so few people are trained for it.

You probably know what the fear is like. Before giving an oral report, do you feel nervous? Do your palms sweat? Is your throat dry? Do you get ''butterflies'' in your stomach? These feelings are natural physical responses to any situation in which you risk something. Many famous athletes, singers, and actors admit to these same feelings even after years of successful performance.

You can understand these physical sensations if you think about an animal in a frightening situation. The animal must be ready for one of two things—*flight or fight*. It must defend itself or run away. Either action requires great physical energy, and the animal's body prepares itself. The heart rate goes up. Breathing rate increases. A substance called *adrenalin* is pumped into the bloodstream. Perspiration increases. The animal feels different because the flight-or-fight response has changed its body slightly to prepare it for whatever happens.

The same thing happens to you when you feel fear. Stage fright is not imaginary. The feelings are very real. In fact, as many athletes know, stage fright can be beneficial. By preparing you for whatever happens, stage fright can give you an edge—something extra that helps you perform. Even experienced public speakers feel these changes. Some even worry if they are not nervous. If you feel uneasy before a speech, do not worry. You are perfectly normal!

SPEAK UP!   Think of a situation in which you were frightened. Share your story with the class. Include as much detail as you can about your physical reaction. When the class has completed the presentations, make a list of similarities among the incidents.

The risk in a public speaking situation is easy to understand. If you are like other people, you are worried that your speech won't be successful. Most students ask, ''What if I make a fool of myself?''

It may be hard to realize, but millions of speeches are given every week in this country. If you are reasonably well prepared, your speech will be fine. Others will listen and respond if you speak to them honestly and openly.

It is impossible to know exactly what the future holds for you. Many people who thought they would never give a speech have been surprised to find that public speaking is an important part of their lives. You never know when you will be faced with a situation like the one described in "Picture This. . .". If you speak out, you will have the satisfaction of making your opinion known. If you refuse to speak, you may always wonder if you could have made a difference.

There are several things to remember that will help reduce your negative feelings:

1. Everyone else feels very much as you do.
2. If you can choose the specific topic, find a subject you feel comfortable with.
3. If you are prepared, you probably know more about your subject than anyone else in the room.
4. You have important, worthwhile information and opinions.
5. The opportunities outweigh the risks.
6. Experience increases your chances of success.

CHOOSING TO SPEAK

If you choose to speak, you can recognize the opportunity by noting four things. First is there a problem or goal? If there is a reason to speak, there must be a problem to be solved, a goal to be met, or a question to be answered. This part of the situation gives a speech *purpose*. Second, there must be an *audience*, a group of people who are interested in the problem. The audience is usually a group whose opinions or actions could help solve the problem or meet the goal. Third is the *message*. The message is the speech. It is made up of information and opinion organized into an understandable form. It also includes everything the audience may see the speaker do or hear the speaker say. The *speaker* is the last part of the speaking situation. When you choose to address a problem or goal by delivering a message to an audience, you become the speaker.

Purpose
A person gives a speech for a reason. The reason might be as simple as honoring someone who is receiving an award or as complex as informing a group of executives about all of the new services they can have through computers. The speech purpose is actually part of the larger situation. The situation involves all the factors surrounding the speech. The location, time, composition of the audience, and the reason for the audience being there—all are parts of the situation.

Audience
The audience is the group of people listening to the speech. Without an audience, there would be no need to speak. The audience's interests and needs affect the topic of a speech and how it is presented. For example, a group of eight-year-olds would not be interested in knowing how to interview for a summer job, but they might be interested in knowing how to make a puppet from common household items.

Speaker   A third element in the speech process is you, the speaker. A speaker is usually asked to speak to a group on a particular occasion because the speaker knows something the group wants to hear. A speaker should analyze his or her knowledge and skills in preparing the speech. The opportunity to share information does have risks. Unless a speaker considers personal strengths and weaknesses, he or she might not prepare an effective speech.

Message   Once a speaker has analyzed the purpose and audience and has conducted a self-analysis, it is time to compose a message. The message is the content of the speech. What the speaker says and how it is said are parts of the message. How a message is presented is often referred to as the *treatment*. Treatment includes the tone of the speech—is it serious, humorous, angry? It also includes the language used—is it formal, informal, complex, or simple? A message is affected by the nature of the situation and the composition of the audience. A speech that is perfect for one audience and situation might not be for another. A speech on how to build a solar heating unit to conserve energy would be useful for suburban homeowners, but would not interest anyone living in city apartments.

TALK ABOUT IT!   Divide into groups. Using the four elements of public speaking, describe to the class a speaking situation you observed recently. Use these questions to help organize your description.

A. Speaker
1. Who was the speaker?
2. What were the speaker's qualifications and background?
3. Why was the speaker addressing the audience?
4. Did you know anything about the speaker before the speech? If yes, what?
5. How did previous knowledge, or lack of it, affect your expectations?
6. What did you know about the speaker by the end of the speech?

B. Audience
1. Who was in the audience?
2. What did audience members have in common?
3. How did some members of the audience differ from others?
4. What was the audience's attitude toward the topic?
5. Were audience members there voluntarily?

C. Purpose
1. What was the occasion for the speech?
2. Where did the speech take place?
3. When did the speech take place?
4. What was the goal of the speech?

D. Message
1. What was the subject or theme?
2. How did the message relate to the audience?
3. How did the message relate to the situation?
4. Was the subject an appropriate one for the speaker?
5. Was the message written effectively?
6. Was the message delivered effectively?

SUMMARY

Throughout your life you will have many opportunities to use public speaking to your advantage. Living in a democracy, becoming educated, and pursuing a career all make training in public speaking desirable. As you develop your speaking skills, you will learn to cope with the stage fright that all speakers feel at one time or another.

Every speaking opportunity has four parts: the purpose or goal, the audience, the speaker, and the message. Only by considering all four parts of the speaking situation can you recognize the opportunity and prepare a successful speech.

2

Audience & Occasion

Picture This . . .

Local television stations and newspapers are organizing a telethon to locate part-time and full-time jobs for people in the community. Businesses will be asked to list openings with the director of the project. Students and others applying for jobs will be matched with these businesses.

The guidance counselors at your school will select students to give two-minute speeches explaining why young people need jobs. Students will work together on their speeches to avoid duplication. You know why young people need jobs, but you also know that many lack work experience. You need to convince the audience members that they would benefit from employing you and your friends. In order to do this, you must know something about the audience. The following is a list of audience analysis questions you might ask. Number the questions in the order of their importance in preparing the speeches.

- What types of jobs could be filled by young people?
- Is the audience composed of both men and women?
- What types of businesses do audience members represent?
- Have local businesses hired students before?
- What do audience members know about the project?
- What opinions do businesses have of young people as employees?

INTRODUCTION: Audience and Occasion

A speech is given for an audience. Without anyone to listen, there is no reason to speak. You must know your audience and your purpose before composing your message. The audience analysis questions in "Picture This . . ." give you an idea of the questions you should ask. In this lesson you will find out what you need to know about an audience and why. In analyzing an audience, you must answer three general questions:

1. Who is in the audience?
2. Why are these people together?
3. What do the audience members know or think about my topic and about me?

These questions are summarized by three words: *demographics*, *situation*, and *attitudes*. By analyzing these three factors, you will prepare a speech that suits the audience's needs and achieves your purpose.

DEMOGRAPHICS

How many students in your class have jobs? What is the average age of your classmates? How many of your classmates are female? Male? How many of your classmates have brothers? How many have sisters? How many of each?

Answers to these questions will help you know a little more about the average student in your class. Facts and information about people are referred to as *demographic data*. A demographic analysis usually reveals the following facts about an audience for a speech:

Age   Religion
Gender   Political background
Occupation   Ethnic or cultural background
Educational background

Very few members of an audience are the same on all counts, but most have some characteristics in common. Your purpose in learning the demographics of an audience is to give examples or to make arguments that will interest them. If the audience members share many traits, your job is easier than if they do not. For example, in writing this book, we assume our readers are students. If we define *student* as "one who studies," or "one who attends a school," then we have an audience of millions. But we still have not learned much about the members of our audience. Students in cities have different lifestyles from students in rural communities. However, students in both large cities and small towns probably listen to some of the same music and follow some of the same fashions. As we select our examples, we attempt to match them to the interests, experiences, and lifestyles of students throughout the United States. Some examples may have little meaning for some students, but overall, there will be something everyone can identify with. As a speaker, you want to find something that everyone can understand.

If you fail to learn about an audience's background, you can prepare the wrong message. Several years ago, a well-known national politician appeared in a Kansas community of approximately 120,000 people. Because most people associate farming with Kansas, the speaker assumed farming should be the major focus of his speech. Most audience members, however, were doctors, lawyers, teachers, business people, and homemakers. Many of them had never been on a farm and did not identify with the speaker's message about farming. The speech was well written and well delivered, but it was not successful. It did not appeal to the needs or interests of the audience. Even an experienced speaker can mis-analyze an audience! In order to avoid a similar mistake, you should always conduct a demographic analysis of your audience.

ACTIVITY 1   Find out the following about your classmates and then write a description of the "average" member of your class.

1. How many play a musical instrument?

2. How many have jobs?

3. How many have a driver's license?

4. How many cook?

5. What is the average number of hours spent watching television per week?

6. What is the average age?

7. How many students have brothers or sisters?

8. How many participate in one or more sports?

9. How many belong to a club or organization?

10. How many have travelled outside the state?

Age   Age affects what you know and the experiences you have had. Older audiences have more life experiences and education, and speakers can choose from a broader range of examples. While it is possible to discuss the same topic with audiences of different ages, you must treat the topic differently for each. If you were trying to defend your favorite rock group to a friend who has a different favorite and to a seventy-year-old person who dislikes rock music, you would use different arguments. With your friend you would compare the quality of the music and the lyrics. With the older person, you would defend rock music in general. You might compare the group with one that was popular thirty or forty years ago.

Age affects topic treatment in another way. For instance, you must use simple language for young children. Also, your speech must be short because a child's attention span is very short.

SPEAK UP!   Prepare two brief introductions (one minute each) of your best friend. One is to be given to an older person and the other to a classmate. Present the introductions to the class and explain why you prepared each as you did.

Gender   Gender is another word for classification according to sex. What percentage of the audience is male? What percentage is female? Most audiences are composed of both men and women, but occasionally you will find an all-male or an all-female audience. Depending on the speech topic you choose, the composition of your audience may be a significant factor in how you prepare your speech.

Many topics don't require special treatment. For example, if you were to give a speech on the history of computer games, you could give the same speech to a predominantly female or predominantly male audience. However, consider a speech topic such as one on the federal law requiring equal treatment for girls' and boys' athletic programs within a public school. A female audience might be more sympathetic when they hear about possible sex discrimination, while a male audience might be concerned about the law's impact on boys' athletic programs. Being aware of the composition of your audience would help you prepare an effective speech for such a topic, including examples to which your audience can relate.

TALK ABOUT IT! Work in a group to prepare a short opinion poll. Half of the group members should give it to males, the other half to females. Compile the results. Are there differences between male and female responses? Examples of questions are:

1. What is your favorite sport?

2. Should all students be required to take computer science?

3. Should men get custody of children in divorce settlements?

4. Should women be allowed in combat?

Present your findings to the class and compare your results with those of the other groups.

Occupation A person's occupation often influences his or her lifestyle. Lifestyle, in turn, affects interests and attitudes. For example, someone working on an assembly line has a different view of unions and occupational safety than does a lawyer. A person's occupation affects income and social standing. Both of those factors determine where a person lives, what a person does during leisure time, or even how a person dresses.

In the example given about the speaker discussing farming with city dwellers, occupation affected attitudes toward the topic. A speaker could discuss the general topic of farming with audiences in New York City or Los Angeles as well as with audiences in rural Iowa or Nebraska. However, the speaker's topic development would differ for each set of audiences. The topic of improving farm policy to increase farmers' incomes would not appeal to people in New York City, but a topic concerned with the effects of farm policy on food prices would.

Occupation also influences a person's vocabulary. Each occupation has its own special language, known as *jargon*. Jargon is not always understood by outsiders. When you go to a computer store, you might hear people discussing "megabytes" or "BASIC" or "head crashes." Or you might hear a baseball fan say that someone pitches a "shut-out" or "fanned" six batters. These terms are examples of jargon. A speaker addressing an audience composed of people in the same occupation can use jargon. However, a speaker cannot use jargon for a general audience without explaining these terms.

ACTIVITY 2 Watch several television shows that include characters in different occupations. Make a list of the jargon terms for each occupation. If you have a job, list the jargon terms used in that job. Select three examples from your list and define them so that everyone in the class will know what they mean.

Educational Background Closely related to occupation is educational background, because people's educational backgrounds influence their occupations. Some occupations require education beyond a college degree, while others require special training instead of formal schooling. Barbers and beauticians must have special training, and in some cases, must pass a state test. However, they do not necessarily need a college degree in order to succeed in their careers.

A person's educational background also affects knowledge, vocabulary, and attitudes. This does not mean a person with a high school or college diploma knows more than someone without one. It simply means the person knows about different subjects.

A speaker must know something about the audience's educational background to avoid speaking either "above their heads" or "down" to them. Think about a time when someone spoke to you as if you were a child. You were probably insulted or angry. A speaker does not want to create such feelings.

Religious Background

The United States was founded on the principle of religious freedom. Because of this, Americans may choose to belong to any religion or even no religion at all. It is often said the two topics that should never be discussed are religion and politics. Religion, especially, is very personal. It often affects a person's beliefs about social issues such as drinking, war, or divorce. On many topics, religion may have no influence, but on controversial issues, speakers must take into account the religious backgrounds of the audience members. Speakers should be very sensitive to these facts and should avoid saying anything that could be interpreted as an insult to another person's religion.

Ethnic and Cultural Background

The United States is often called a melting pot because it is composed of people from many countries. Just as a speaker must be aware of the many religious groups in this country, a speaker must also be aware of ethnic or cultural differences. Once again, common sense is the key.

SITUATION

Knowing who is in your audience is often not enough. You must also know why the audience members have gathered together to hear you speak. As you prepare your speech, you should ask several questions about the speaking situation:

1. What is the occasion?
2. What do audience members have in common?
3. What is the physical location of the speech?
4. How long should you speak?
5. What comes before and after your speech?

When you combine answers to these questions with demographic data, you will be better able to write a speech to meet the audience's needs and interests.

What Is the Occasion?

A speaker needs to know why an audience is gathered together. Is the occasion for the speech a school assembly? Is it a regular meeting of an organization? Is the speech part of a holiday celebration? Whatever the occasion, it affects the content. If a person is speaking at a special event, such as a celebration of Dr. Martin Luther King, Jr.'s birthday, the subject must be consistent with the purpose for the group's meeting. A speech describing Dr. King's contributions in civil rights would be more appropriate than one discussing accomplishments of American Olympic athletes.

What Do Audience Members Have in Common?

Audiences are composed of individuals, but those individuals often share a reason for being present at a speech. If a person is speaking to an organization, the audience is there because they hold membership or have an interest in the organization. A speech can be designed to appeal to those interests or to the organization's goals.

When a famous speaker is featured at an assembly or gathering, it is often assumed that audience members have chosen to attend the speech. In such situations, they are a voluntary audience. When students attend a school assembly, they are an involuntary audience. How does your attitude toward a required assembly or meeting compare to your attitude toward attending a concert or football game? Whether audience members attend a speech freely can affect their attitudes toward the topic and the speaker. A speaker facing an involuntary audience has a more difficult task. The speaker must work harder to interest the audience in listening.

What Is the Physical Location of the Speech?

The physical surroundings for a speech often influence how a speech is delivered. A speech given in a classroom in front of twenty-five people will be less formal than one given in an auditorium seating two thousand people. In the latter case, the speaker will be physically distant from the audience and will have to use a microphone. Using a microphone can affect how the speaker delivers the speech. It can also reduce the speaker's ability to move about. Speakers who look stiff often sound stiff.

The location can also create problems for the speaker. If a speech is held outdoors, the noises and distractions cannot be controlled. The speaker must adapt by speaking louder or by pausing until the noise stops. If people are standing in a crowded park, they will not be willing to listen as long as if they were seated in a comfortable auditorium.

ACTIVITY 3

Look at the room in which you will be speaking for this class. Write a brief description of the features that will help you give the speech and those that will create distractions or problems.

A speaker must know about a setting for practical reasons as well. If you want to show slides during a speech, you must be sure there is a screen and an electrical outlet or extension cord. If you plan to use charts, you must know something about the size of the room so the charts will be large enough for everyone to see.

The size of the location affects the size of the audience. The larger the room, the more people it will hold. The more people present, the less personal your presentation will be.

As a speaker you should feel comfortable with the physical location. Before the day of the speech, ask questions about the room. Be sure to arrive for a speech early enough to "get a feel" for the room.

How Long Should You Speak?

The length of your speech should be determined by several factors. One is whether or not you are the only speaker. Few audiences will listen to two or three hour-long speeches. If you are the only speaker but speak at the end of a long agenda of announcements, awards, or other activities, your speech should be shorter than if you were the only person on the agenda.

It is always appropriate to ask the person who invited you for a time estimate for the speech. Usually that person knows how long the entire program will be and what the group expects. Be sure to follow time guidelines. They are given for a reason. If you speak longer than is suggested, you will lose the audience's interest. You might also upset the group's schedule of activities or deprive someone else of the time he or she expected to have.

What Comes Before and After Your Speech?

You need to know as much as possible about the events that precede and follow your speech. It is often helpful to refer to them during your speech. If a musical group performs before your speech, you can mention something about their performance as an example of a point you want to make. This lets the audience know you are part of the total program. You also need to know what comes before and after your speech because you do not want to duplicate another person's part of the program. Nothing is worse than listening to someone else give your speech.

Often speeches are followed by question-and-answer periods. Find out if there will be an opportunity for audience members to ask questions. If there is, you do not need as much detail in the speech.

ATTITUDES

Several times we have referred to audience attitude or beliefs. An *attitude* or *belief* is something we think is true, right, or acceptable. Our beliefs and attitudes develop over time. Our families, teachers, religious leaders, friends, and life experiences influence our beliefs. A speaker must know about an audience's beliefs before composing a speech. Audiences are characterized as agreeing, disagreeing, or neutral depending on their initial attitudes toward you and your subject.

If an audience shares your beliefs, you will prepare a different message than if the audience doesn't. If you are trying to convince a friend to attend one movie and your friend wants to attend another, your conversation will be different than if you and your friend want to see the same movie. In the first instance, both of you will have to agree on which movie to see before you plan how you will get there or what time you will go. In the second situation your conversation will be much briefer.

If a speaker addresses a group that holds differing views, the goal will be to persuade the group. If a speaker addresses an audience with similar views, the goal will be to inform rather than persuade. If the audience's attitudes are different from your own, you might not be able to change their minds entirely. Instead you might want to set the goal of encouraging them to understand your position.

A neutral audience is one that knows little about the topic before hearing your speech or is undecided on the issue. For this type of audience your purpose is to assist in creating an attitude or belief. It is important to understand why the audience has no prior information or why it is unable to reach a conclusion. It could be that a topic is a new concern within a community or is the result of new research. It is also possible that audience members have several attractive alternatives from which to choose and need more information about their relative merits.

You learn about an audience's cultural background and beliefs by asking questions of others—locate people who know something about the group. You may also gather information by reading about the group. If you are asked to address a group of AFS students (American Field Services), you can read AFS literature for a better understanding of the audience.

Part of being a successful persuader is understanding your own beliefs and how they developed. If you realize your beliefs are a part of experiences you have had which are not shared by audience members, you may describe those experiences. By knowing how you developed your opinions, the audience will be more likely to understand your position even if they don't agree with it.

It is important to respect the beliefs of other people. A speaker should not ridicule, insult, or criticize an audience's beliefs.

ACTIVITY 4   What are your attitudes about the following topics?

1. Letter grades for assignments
2. The drinking age
3. Working mothers
4. Donating organs when you die
5. The death penalty
6. Balancing economic and ecological needs

Why do you have these attitudes? What experiences would cause others to have different attitudes? Select one of the topics and list or describe everything that has influenced your belief.

DIFFERENT AUDIENCES

As you have read about demographics, situation, and attitude, you might have thought, "What does this have to do with me? I know that all my speeches will be given to my classmates and the teacher."

At some point in your life, you may give speeches to other audiences. Even speeches to your classmates require you to think of their interests. The teacher will place a time limit on your speeches. The physical surroundings will affect your presentations. Your speeches will be evaluated, and you must meet the requirements for evaluation. Even in a classroom setting, you must analyze the audience, the situation, and the audience's beliefs. The activities throughout this lesson will assist you in preparing speeches for audiences both in and out of the classroom.

SUMMARY

The audience is the most important part of a speech. You give a speech for the audience's benefit. Before writing a speech, a speaker must learn about the audience's background or demographics, the occasion for the speech, and the audience's attitudes about the topic and the speaker.

Audience and occasion analysis require research. The speaker must ask questions or conduct some type of library research to find out as much as possible about the audience and the occasion. Unless a speaker analyzes the audience and occasion, the topic and treatment might not be appropriate.

3

Speech Purposes

Picture This...

You are a member of a committee that is organizing a program on the importance of supporting our Olympic teams. Your guest speaker was a gold-medal winner in the 1992 Olympics. Although the guest, a woman in her teens, is well known, many people will not be familiar with her accomplishments. Your committee must develop an introduction that will precede her speech. People from all over the city will attend. Your guest's speech is on "Supporting the Goals of Our Nation's Youth." Which of the following introductions should your group choose?

A. One student will give a three- or five-minute speech listing the guest's accomplishments and providing a short biography.
B. Three students will prepare three short clever speeches that will humorously "roast" the guest speaker before her presentation.
C. The mayor will be invited to talk about the history of the Olympics.
D. Your committee will produce a slide show of the guest's recent accomplishments.
E. A student will read a recent magazine article written about the guest.

INTRODUCTION: Speech Purposes

Whenever you prepare to speak in front of a group, you must have a specific purpose in mind. If you do not, you may have trouble deciding exactly what to say. More important, the audience may have trouble understanding exactly what you said.

In "Picture This . . . ," the committee had to identify the purpose of the introduction before it decided what kind of introduction to give the guest speaker. Did the committee want to impress the audience? Should the introduction make the audience laugh? Should the introduction convince the audience to listen? Should the introduction do all three? Only by answering questions like these can the committee make an intelligent decision about the introduction.

Identifying a speech purpose is an important early step in speech preparation. Once you have identified the problem and the audience, you must find the speech purpose.

SPEAKING TO ENTERTAIN

A speech that tries only to gain and keep the audience's attention is a speech to entertain. The speech to entertain seems to have a simple purpose, but entertaining people is much more difficult than it seems. Consider how hard it is to entertain a group of students during the last hour of the school day on Friday.

One of the traditional forms of the speech to entertain is the after-dinner speech. After-dinner speeches are often relaxing, witty, humorous, and informal. As the name suggests, they are given after formal dinners as a light entertainment. One man famous for his after-dinner speeches was Mark Twain. Twain's speeches depended not only on his humor but also on his unique ability to tell a story. Some of you may have attended an athletic banquet or a banquet sponsored by an organization. If you have, you most likely heard an after-dinner speaker who told humorous stories about the people or activities involved.

Other examples of speeches to entertain are the celebrity roasts which appear on television. These speeches are designed only to make us laugh and pass the time pleasantly. The famous people who are "roasted" know that the remarks made about them are only made in fun. We in the audience expect only light, happy speeches.

However a speech to entertain is not always humorous. You may recall hearing someone tell a story that was frightening or unusual—and also very entertaining. Perhaps you have attended a travelogue, a presentation of pictures accompanied by a speech. While travelogues are informative, their primary function is often entertainment. People attend them for recreation and pleasure. Speeches to entertain are the least common type of speech. Most of the strategies for speech development that you will be learning can be applied to entertainment speeches.

ACTIVITY 1   Identify and list ten topics you think people your age would find entertaining. Compare your list to others in the class. In a class discussion, identify the "Top Ten Topics" for your age group.

TALK ABOUT IT!   Select a short joke or a funny story. In groups of four to six, take turns telling your jokes or stories. Each group should select one member to tell his or her selection to the class.

By now, you have probably realized that something entertaining is usually something new. How often can you be entertained by the same joke? Even the most entertaining after-dinner speech depends in part on novelty. In other words, a speech to entertain often presents new information.

SPEAKING TO INFORM

You are most familiar with the speech to inform. By now you have probably heard many classroom lectures. These lectures were really informative speeches.

Informative speeches are also important outside school. In business, for example, people often must inform large and small groups about policies, sales programs, safety campaigns, or financial reports. In fact, many business meetings are really a series of informative speeches given by one person or by several people.

In an informative speech, the audience hears about a new subject or new information on a common subject. You might be interested in unusual, new topics like these:

New uses for computers in the classroom
A completely automated factory

Fuel made from sunflower oil
The invention of America's top video game

On the other hand, some "old" subjects are always interesting if you can provide the audience with new information:

Vampire legends
Atlantis

Sharks
Baseball

Information you present should be new *to your audience*. Giving an informative speech on stars to a group of astronomers requires a different kind of information than a speech on the same subject given to a student science club. The astronomers would expect technical information. They would understand the terms. They would probably want to know about new research in astronomy. The science club, however, would want general information. They would want new terms defined. They would not expect anything more than a basic explanation of the subject.

ACTIVITY 2   Think about recent television shows you have seen or magazine articles you have read. Identify five "hot" topics that are new and exciting to the public. Write a short explanation of why the public is interested in the topic.

SPEAKING TO PERSUADE

A speech that is intended to change the attitudes or behaviors of the audience is a speech to persuade. The speech to persuade is probably the most challenging kind of speech because it frequently concerns subjects of very great importance to both speaker and audience.

Persuasive speeches are given every day. Note the opportunities for persuasion in these situations:

Going on a job interview

Borrowing a car

Explaining why you were late for class

Working on a fund drive for a local charity

Arguing about the season's best new movie

What are the risks and opportunities in each situation?

When you try to convince your parents, teacher, or employer to let you do something, you are giving an informal persuasive speech. A sales presentation is a formal persuasive speech. The salesperson wants your attitude toward the product to change so that your behavior will change and you will buy the product.

The most common persuasive speeches are those given by political speakers. Often political speeches concern a particular candidate. Even more often, the speakers seek to persuade you about controversial—even emotional—issues. These speeches usually require more thought and preparation than any others.

ACTIVITY 3   For each category listed below, identify a controversial subject that might be a topic for a persuasive speech.

1. The students in your school

2. A community group

3. Residents of your state

4. A senior citizens' group

5. A group of minority business leaders

6. A group of single parents

Overlapping Purposes   While the division of speech purposes into entertainment, informative, and persuasive is convenient, speeches seldom demonstrate only one of the three purposes. Usually, all three purposes exist in one speech with one of the purposes being most important.

Consider a speaker whose purpose is to persuade the audience to support a new community athletic program. The speaker will probably want to be entertaining so the audience will pay attention and enjoy the speech. In addition, the speaker will have to give the audience information about the subject. Without the information, the audience might not understand its importance. Still, entertainment and information are not the primary purposes. Since the speaker is seeking support for the new program, the speech will not include entertainment or information unless it helps persuade the audience.

If the speech purpose is to inform, persuasion is still important. A speaker who informs must be believed, so informative speeches must also persuade the audience that the speaker is knowledgeable and trustworthy.

ACTIVITY 4 Want ads seem to have one purpose—to inform the reading public about the availability of jobs, services, and merchandise. Frequently, want ads must also be entertaining to get the reader's attention and persuasive to convince the reader to buy, sell, or apply. Rewrite these simple want ads so they are entertaining, informative, and persuasive at the same time.

For Sale: Small, older house not far from the city. Three bedrooms. Garden space. Fireplace. Priced in the low 50s. Bryan Real Estate 555-4647.

Cars for Sale: Smitty's Used Car Lot offers good prices on sports cars, family cars, and trucks. Call 555-1895.

Positions now available for mature teens seeking summer employment. The city swimming pools are now taking applications for jobs as lifeguards, cashiers, pool maintenance persons, and managers. Write P.O. Box 123.

Hidden Agenda Speech purposes aren't always openly identified. Perhaps you have been invited to a party which you thought would be entertaining only to find out that you were being persuaded to join a group or buy a product. When a speech has a purpose which is intentionally unstated or hidden behind another purpose, the speech has a *hidden agenda.*

Sometimes the hidden agenda may be to inform. What seem to be entertaining speeches often are full of information that a speaker wants the audience to learn. This is especially true of speeches given to children. Even children's television shows sometimes disguise informational purposes with entertainment.

Hiding your purpose may not be a good idea. There may be several problems. Your hidden purpose may miss the audience entirely, or your audience may perceive the hidden purpose and disregard it.

STATING YOUR PURPOSE

Whether your primary purpose is to entertain, inform, or persuade, you must state the purpose for both yourself and your audience. The statement of purpose controls your speech preparation and narrows your topic. A good purpose statement has two important characteristics.

First, a good purpose statement is phrased in terms of the audience. What do you want the audience reaction to be? If you do not know what you want from the audience, how will you know what to say and how to say it? For example:

The purpose of this speech is to give a humorous review of the swimming season for team members and fans. (entertain)

The purpose of this speech is to update the new students on recent changes in school rules and policies. (inform)

The purpose of this speech is to convince the club members that selling calendars is a good way to raise money. (persuade)

Notice that each purpose statement specifies the *audience* (swim team members and fans, new students, and club members), the *subject* (the swim season, new rules and policies, and fund raising), and the *desired result* (review, update, and convince). In other words, these purpose statements relate the audience to the subject by identifying the speaker's purpose.

Second, a good purpose statement limits the speech by limiting the subject. When you prepare a speech, you must decide what you will and will not include. Without an idea of your purpose, you cannot make good decisions. Suppose you are going to give an informative speech on cars to a driver education class. A purpose statement like ''I'm going to tell the class about cars'' is useless. It does not limit the subject nor help you prepare. You do not know whether to cover gas mileage, car care, or racing. If you are unsure of your purpose, the audience is likely to be confused, too. A good purpose statement (like ''The purpose of this speech is to show that simple car maintenance done at home can save money'') narrows the subject. Now you know you will cover gas mileage only because it improves with car maintenance. You will not talk about racing at all. Because you do not have to consider all information about cars, the speech is easier to prepare.

ACTIVITY 5 Rewrite each of these purpose statements:

1. The purpose of this speech is to tell people something about the death penalty.

2. The purpose of this speech is to talk about dancing.

3. The purpose of this speech is to complain about how employers treat their employees.

4. The purpose of this speech is to tell the school board about things going on in school.

Be sure to specify the audience, the subject, and the desired result.

Thesis Statements Since the purpose statement sounds a bit awkward in the speech itself, you convert it to a *thesis statement*. A thesis statement is simply your point of view on the subject reduced to a single sentence. A thesis narrows your speech topic and states your position precisely. Note the differences between this purpose statement and thesis statement:

Purpose Statement: "The purpose of this speech is to convince the club members that selling calendars is a good way to raise money."

Thesis Statement: "Calendar sales return high profits without a big investment."

A thesis statement is the one statement that summarizes the speaker's position. It is necessary for three reasons:

1. A thesis is expected by the audience. People have learned to expect a thesis early in a speech. If it is missing, the listeners' expectations are not met.
2. A thesis helps the audience follow your ideas. If you do not state your position early in the speech, some of your points might not make sense to your audience.
3. A thesis forces you to stick to one subject. If your thesis is ''Doing simple auto maintenance at home can save you money,'' you know not to talk about the recent auto show or the Indianapolis 500.

ACTIVITY 6 Rewrite these purpose statements as thesis statements:

"The purpose of this speech is to tell students how to apply for a job."

"The purpose of this speech is to entertain you by sharing stories about my summer vacation."

"The purpose of this speech is to convince the school board to purchase new microcomputers."

Evaluation Using the Purpose Statement

The purpose statement is a means of evaluating a speaker's effectiveness. As a member of an audience or as a speaker, you usually judge the effectiveness of a speech. The traditional method of judging is to compare the speaker's intentions with the actual results. If the purpose of the speech is to persuade, then the audience's opinion and behavior should change as intended by the speaker. Likewise, if the purpose of the speech is to inform, then the listeners should know more after the speech than they did before the speech.

When you are an audience member, you can analyze a speech by determining what the speaker did and did not do to accomplish the purpose.

SPEAK UP!

Observe a speech on television or attend a lecture in person. Give a two- to four-minute oral report about the speech and do the following:

1. Identify the speaker's purpose. Was it stated or was it part of a hidden agenda?

2. Determine if the speaker succeeded.

3. Explain the speaker's success or failure by referring to specific materials included in the speech.

SUMMARY

After identifying your audience and defining your problem, you must choose a purpose for your speech: to entertain, inform, or persuade. Even though a speech has one important purpose, it may also exhibit characteristics of the other two speech purposes. Sometimes a speaker hides the purpose of a speech. The speech then has a hidden agenda. Usually the speech purpose is phrased as a thesis statement. A thesis is important in speech preparation, speech presentation, and speech evaluation.

4

Topic Selection

Picture This . . .

You are planning your first speech for your public speaking class. It is a speech to inform. You may speak on any topic so long as it meets the guidelines for an informative speech, but you do not know what topic to select. You have checked with several friends in the class and know what topics they have chosen. You have looked through several magazines, but the good topics have been taken. You are running out of time; you must select a topic yet you can't seem to come up with an idea that appeals to you. Which of the following suggestions should you follow to select a topic?

A. Ask people who took the class last year what topics they had.
B. Make a list of everything you are interested in and select one item from the list as a topic area.
C. Make a list of everything your friends and classmates are interested in and select one of those topics.
D. Ask the school librarian to suggest a topic for which there is a great deal of research material available.
E. Select a topic you know nothing about but have been wanting to learn something about.
F. Take a poll of the people in your class and ask them what they would like to hear a speech about.
G. Randomly select a drawer in the card catalog and take the first subject card you find.

INTRODUCTION: Topic Selection

As a student in a speech class, you will be able to identify with the situation in "Picture This . . ." before your course is over. In a sense, a student in a speech class has a problem with topic selection that most speakers in the "real world" of public speaking do not have. Most speakers are asked to speak because they are experts on a topic. While an expert speaker may have to decide exactly how to discuss a topic, the actual topic area is not chosen from all the possible subjects in a card catalog. Often a speaker is asked to speak on a specific occasion. In this case, a speaker would select a topic appropriate for the situation.

Usually when members of a group ask someone to speak, they do so because there is something they want to hear discussed. Thus, there are three factors that affect a speaker's choice and development of a topic: the speaker's knowledge and interests, the speech situation, and the audience's needs or desires. This lesson will discuss topic selection. You will learn how to select a topic that is interesting to both you and the audience.

SPECIFIC TOPICS

Once you learn as much as possible about the audience and occasion, you must decide what to talk about. In some instances, a topic may be decided for you. Even when this occurs, you still have some decisions to make. You may be assigned a general topic, such as "music videos," but you need to decide exactly what you are going to say on the subject. In other words, what is your specific topic? Look at the following list to see how the topic "music videos" can be made more specific.

General Topic: Music videos
Specific Topics:
1.   What makes a good music video?
2.   The top three music videos of the year (including clips from each)
3.   Music videos hurt our imaginative processes.

To an extent, your choice of a specific topic is guided by your speech purpose. If you were giving an informative speech, which of the three specific topics would be best? Which is more suitable for a persuasive speech? Which topic would be most entertaining? As the music video example suggests, you can adjust a *general* topic to fit any speech purpose by matching the *specific* topic to the purpose you have chosen.

Your choice of speech purpose is affected by the audience and the occasion for the speech. In a speech class, you will be asked to give speeches that meet each of the speech purposes. As you select a specific topic, you should consider the purpose.

ACTIVITY 1   For each of the following general topics, make a list of specific topics to fit each of the three major speech purposes (information, persuasion, entertainment):

1. Physical fitness   2. Television programs   3. Fads

Narrowing a Topic   The process through which you develop a specific topic is known as *narrowing*. A topic is narrowed to fit time requirements, as well as the requirements of purpose, audience, and occasion. If you are a photography buff, you might decide to give an informative speech on that topic. You cannot tell everything you know about photography in a five- to seven-minute speech. You must narrow the topic.

Narrowing should be done first by listing subtopics and then by narrowing them further. Using the photography example, you might first divide the topic into the following categories:

1. History   4. Light
2. Cameras   5. Printmaking
3. Lenses   6. Enlarging

For each of these subtopics, you can list specific, narrower topics. "Cameras," for example, could be narrowed down by listing the types of cameras available for different purposes. Then you could choose a specific type of camera for your topic.

After you select a camera, you must determine what to say about it. You could make a list of all you know about the camera and then decide what you could cover in the time limit. By the time you have written your specific purpose statement, you will have gone through the following steps:

General   1. Photography
2. Major types of cameras
3. Single-lens reflex cameras
Specific   4. Advantages of single-lens reflex cameras

In discussing the single-lens reflex camera, you would have to include subtopics such as how the viewfinder system works, interchangeable lenses, quality of the negatives, and flexibility of use. By narrowing, you can give many details about one small part of a very broad topic.

TALK ABOUT IT!   Divide into groups. Select two of the following topics and narrow them from general topics to subtopics to specific topics. Compare your decisions to those of other groups that selected the same topics.

1. Food   4. Study habits
2. Popular music   5. Current trends
3. Family   6. The environment

FINDING A TOPIC

Unless you are interested in your topic, your audience will not be. One of the first steps in topic selection is to find something that interests you. When a person is invited to give a speech, it is usually on a topic the speaker knows something about. A florist would expect to be asked to speak on flower arranging, for example.

For purposes of this course, you need to determine what topics intrest you. You also need to make a list of topics you know something about. Your teacher may provide you with an interest inventory form. If not, simply list your favorite sports, hobbies, vacation spots, and so on in a notebook, and refer to the list whenever you are asked to perpare a speech.

Not only must you be interested in your topic, you must communicate knowledge of the topic. Before an audience will listen to or believe a speaker, the speaker must be credible or believable. Would you listen to a speaker tell you how to administer CPR (Cardiopulmonary Resuscitation) if the person had never taken a CPR course? Probably not. You would want to be confident the speaker knew what he or she was talking about.

Your credibility is built by relating your personal experiences with the topic and by using supportive materials such as quotations from experts, facts, and statistics. If you select a topic you know something about or know where and how you can learn about it, you will have credibility with your audience.

ANALYZING THE AUDIENCE

Whether you give a speech on an assigned topic or you select your own subject, you should consider audience needs. As you narrow a topic, try to determine what the audience would want to hear. Use what you have learned in this class about audience analysis.

For speeches in class, consider the topics you would find interesting. Since your classmates are similar to you in many ways, they should be interested in some of the same topics. Think of five general topics that interest you. Compare your list with those of your classmates. What five topics appear most frequently? What specific topics can you and your classmates develop from the top five general topics? Use these lists as guidelines for selecting topics for your speeches.

In addition to the audience's interests, you should also consider their knowledge of the topic. We usually listen to speeches to hear new information. If a speaker tells us nothing new, we are disappointed. Everyone has studied the Civil War in school, but few of us have heard a detailed description of the battle at Gettysburg. Even if an audience has general knowledge of a topic, the topic can be narrowed to present new or more detailed information.

A final consideration is the reason for audience members to attend the speech. A group of new students at an orientation meeting expects to hear information that will help them get through the first few days of school. If the students are unfamiliar with the building, the speeches should explain the layout of the building. A speech that does not provide needed information does not meet audience expectations and does not succeed.

ACTIVITY 2   Recall a speech you have heard recently—a class lecture, a classmate's speech, or a speech on television. Did that speech match your interests? Did it provide you with new information? Did it fulfill your needs? Write a short analysis (one page), explaining your answers to these questions.

ANALYZING THE OCCASION

A speaker needs to analyze the occasion for a speech and relate both the general and specific topics to the occasion. In fact, the occasion can guide the development of the specific topic.

One of the authors was invited to be the guest speaker at a meeting of insurance agents. The agents were attending the first session of a course designed to help them become better communicators. The person who invited the author did not have a specific topic in mind. After asking several questions about the course and the audience members' backgrounds as speakers, the author decided the speech should relate to the occasion of the first class period. The specific topic chosen was ''How to get the most out of a course on communication.'' Thus, the speech to the agents explained why communication is important in their lives, how study can improve their skills, and what they could expect from the course. The speaker realized that many of the people would be nervous about giving speeches and that at the first meeting, it was important to relieve some of the anxiety.

The topic was suited to the first day of the course because it set the stage for what was to come and gave the agents a reason for being there. The same topic would not have worked at the third or fourth class.

YOUR OWN POINT OF VIEW

By now you have learned a great deal about audience needs. This does not mean that you should tell audience members only what you think they want to hear. You should also express your own particular attitudes about a topic. Remember, you must demonstrate interest in the topic if you expect to gain your listeners' attention. If you do not agree with the audience's position, that does not mean you must ignore your own position. You need to balance your position with the audience's in preparing your speech.

SPEAK UP! Select one of the following general topics. First, narrow it to fit a two- to three-minute speech. Present the speech to a small group of your classmates. After all the speeches are presented, discuss how well they suited the audience needs, how they included the speakers' points of view, and how well they met the limits of time.

1. Cable television
2. Sports
3. Amusement parks
4. Holidays
5. Natural resources

6. Homework
7. Colors
8. Art
9. Hobbies
10. Computer technology

SUMMARY

A speech is about something. Unless you have something to talk about, there is no reason to speak. As a speech student, you will have freedom to select a topic. If you are called upon to give a speech because you know a great deal about a topic, you naturally have some restrictions. However, in both instances you should consider your interests and knowledge, audience analysis factors, and occasion analysis in selecting a topic.

A speech must be prepared to fit time limits. The process of focusing a topic to fit the time, as well as the purpose, is known as narrowing. A speaker should go through an organized system of listing subtopics under a general heading until a specific topic is chosen that meets personal interests, audience and occasion needs, and fits the time limits.

5

Audience Response

Picture This . . .

You are one of three students who are reporting to a science class on magazine articles about recent discoveries in biology. Your report is the last one. One-half of your grade is based on the content of your report. The other half is based on your manner of presentation. The first two students have completed their reports. During the last report, you noticed that several students in the back of the room were talking. Some others had begun to doodle on their notebooks and gaze out the window. One student fell asleep. Your subject is similar to the other two speeches. You have prepared well for your speech; you have a complete outline, a handout, and some pictures to show. Several of your friends are in the class. As you walk to the front of the class, the talking in the back of the room becomes louder. What do you do?

A. Stand facing the class and remain quiet until everyone's attention is on you.
B. Ask the teacher to stop the talking.
C. Make a humorous comment about the sleeping student, hoping that the humor will get the attention of the students.
D. Start your speech in a loud, clear voice.
E. Abandon your outline and begin with the handouts and pictures.
F. Joke with your friends to get the attention of the class.
G. Refuse to give the speech.
H. Give the speech exactly as you have prepared it.

INTRODUCTION: Audience Response

When you are having a conversation with other people, how do you know they are listening to you? You may receive comments on what you said. If they respond to your questions and if they are following your train of thought, they are probably listening. You watch those who aren't talking. If they are looking at you and nodding their heads, they are probably listening. On the other hand, if you address a comment to someone and do not get a response, you may have to change your communication in order to get and keep the attention of the group. You may change subjects, speak more loudly, or make a face.

Whether or not you think about it, you are using *feedback* to help your communication. By noting the responses of your listeners and changing your conversation to adapt to their responses, you are using feedback to improve your effectiveness.

When you are the listener rather than the speaker, you are still using feedback. Your comments, posture, and gestures all tell the speaker how you are reacting to the speech.

In "Picture This . . .," you were presented with a problem that most speakers face at one time or another—a bored, restless audience. As a speaker, will you change your message to solve this problem? That is a risk, but so is speaking to a bored audience. Using feedback is a natural part of your speech, but it is not always easy. Easy or not, it is one of the most important parts of effective public speaking.

FEEDBACK

When you send a message, you expect some kind of response. You decide if the message is understood by the nature of the response. Such a response is called *feedback*.

For being such a natural part of communication, feedback is a relatively new term. The term *feedback* describes any part of a system's (speaker's) product (message) that is returned to the system (speaker) to enable it to modify further products (messages). That rather complicated definition means that feedback is a method for checking that a desired result is being achieved.

At a very simple level, imagine the young baseball pitcher who has just learned to throw a curve ball. He wants to check to see if he is throwing the ball correctly. He can ask the coach how well he did. The coach may then give him feedback about his stance, his movements, and his hold on the baseball. The pitcher can get more feedback by pitching to the team's best batter. If the batter swings at three pitches and misses three times, the strikeout is proof that the desired result has been achieved. The strikeout is feedback because it is a method for a system (the pitcher) to check itself and to modify itself if needed.

An automobile dashboard is an excellent example of mechanical feedback. The driver, who becomes part of the system, observes all the dials, gauges, and meters to keep the system (the car) producing the desired result—cruising at 55 miles per hour. If the speedometer drops to 48 m.p.h., the driver presses the accelerator to correct the system. If the temperature gauge shows too much heat or the oil light goes on, the driver pulls into a service station to check the problem. Experienced drivers can even get feedback simply by listening to the engine and touching the steering wheel.

All of the mechanisms that inform the driver that the car is working properly are called *feedback loops*. A feedback loop is simply a means of providing a response. For speakers, feedback loops provide responses that enable them to judge the effectiveness of their messages. Based on the information from the feedback loop, a speaker can alter and adjust messages to satisfy the audience's needs. For instance, if a speaker notices that audience members are straining to hear, the speaker can speak more loudly. The public speaker uses three feedback loops in preparing, presenting, and evaluating a speech. The diagram in Figure 1 explains each loop.

Figure 1. Three Feedback Loops

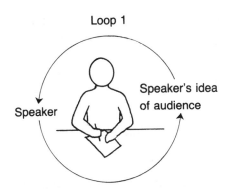

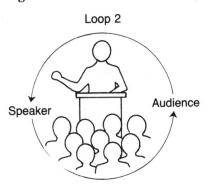

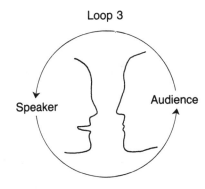

Pre-Speech

The speaker anticipates the audience's response and creates a speech that will be clear and effective.

Presentation

The speaker presents the speech. As the audience responds, the speaker alters the speech to improve effectiveness.

Post-Speech

The speaker judges the effectiveness of the speech by observing the audience's behavior and listening to comments. The speaker uses the observation to help construct future speeches for the audience.

ACTIVITY 1 Choose one of the following. Explain how it is part of a feedback loop and what process it tries to control:

1. A thermostat
2. A pop quiz
3. A tire pressure gauge
4. The sound on a video game

5. A metal detector
6. A compass
7. A bathroom scale
8. A dressing mirror

Anticipating Feedback In the examples you have read so far, feedback is part of an operating system. Ideally feedback in public speaking begins long before the speech itself is delivered. As you prepare your speech, you can simulate feedback so your preparation will be as effective as possible.

You can do this by knowing who the audience is and what the speech's purpose is. If you know these two things, then you can imagine your audience's response to what you have to say. Will the speech produce the desired result? If not, consider how your message can be modified to improve results. By imagining the audience and adjusting your message, you have already established a feedback loop.

Consider this example: Assume you want permission from the librarian to have study groups in the library. Begin by knowing what you want—permission for thirty minutes of group work, which includes quiet discussion among group members. Consider your audience—will the librarian respond favorably? Does the librarian think students are responsible and well-behaved people? Which arguments would likely persuade the librarian: The library is the best place to study? The students will enjoy themselves? The students must study together on some subjects? The public library allows group work? By anticipating the librarian's response, you might prepare an effective case for group work in the library. If, on the other hand, you do not consider your potential audience, you may say the wrong thing and fail to gain the desired effect.

By centering your concerns on the potential audience, you help yourself answer questions about subject matter, content, and style of presentation.

TALK ABOUT IT!   Divide into groups. Assume you are giving a speech on music. From the lists below choose specific audiences for each topic. Discuss how the audiences would respond. Be prepared to justify your choices.

Topic	Audience
1. Trends in music in the coming year	a. A senior citizen group
2. Songs that deal with social issues	b. A meeting of orchestra members
3. The growing popularity of country music	c. A group of children, eleven to twelve years old
4. Music of the 1930s compared to music of the 1980s	d. A conference on problems and issues affecting teenagers
5. The hot new groups in teen music	e. A parent-teacher group meeting
6. The influence of rock music and musicians on today's young people	f. A psychology class
7. Classical music	g. A speech class

SPEAK UP!   Cut out a magazine or newspaper advertisement that interests you. Look in magazines and newspapers aimed at specific groups such as women, young people, children, hobbyists, etc. You will soon see that ads are designed to appeal to different groups. A home computer ad, for example, uses cost and educational benefits to appeal to adults, but it uses cartoon characters to appeal to children. Develop a three-minute speech on the ad you selected. Cover the following in your speech: At what audience is the advertisement aimed? What does the advertiser want the audience to think, feel, or do? What specific things did the advertiser do to get the audience to respond?

Before you give the speech to the class, try out your three-minute speech on another student. Get the student's advice on your speech. Do the same for him or her. Make necessary changes before you give the speech to the class.

Using Feedback During the Speech

After you have prepared a speech, you have completed one feedback loop and are ready to start the next one. While you are giving the speech, you can still use the responses from the audience to "fine tune" your speech so it achieves your goals.

Many public speaking situations allow open questions from the audience. In such a case, direct verbal feedback can help the speaker. If questions seem to focus on one particular subject, you may spend more time on that subject than you had planned. If a question shows misunderstanding, you can clear it up before the speech is finished.

Frequently, however, a public speaking situation allows no direct verbal feedback. In such cases the speaker must rely on observing clues given off by the audience. A speaker who notices several people leaning forward to hear better will probably start speaking louder. A number of people craning their necks might indicate the audience has trouble seeing, and a thoughtful speaker will make the materials and presentation more visible.

"Reading" an audience's feedback requires few skills you do not already have. What it does require is thoughtfulness, attention, and willingness to adjust to audience response. For example, during the final round of a debate tournament, one of the debaters began an important speech. A few moments after the beginning, a marching band began practicing outside the building, and the music blared in through the open windows. Hearing the music, the speaker looked at the audience and noted several people scowling, others straining to hear. Without stopping the speech, the student spoke more loudly, walked to the side of the room, and shut the windows. Returning to the front of the room, the speaker was greeted by smiles of approval and amusement. The debater simply used common sense. The audience's reactions to the music obviously meant that the speaker's effects would be diminished. Closing the windows and speaking more loudly were logical solutions. The smiles indicated the "system" was back on track.

Most examples of feedback are less dramatic than this one. Still, it illustrates what effective speakers can do. Reaching an audience may call for changes in voice, posture, organization, or any other part of a speech as the speech is being delivered.

ACTIVITY 2

If you were a speaker observing the following responses, how would you interpret them? Write your interpretation of each one. Some may have more than one answer.

1. Nodding head
2. Shaking head
3. Sitting on the front edge of a chair and leaning forward
4. Folding arms across the chest
5. Placing both hands behind head, elbows out
6. Drooping eyelids
7. Scowling
8. Staring down
9. Staring up

Feedback and Evaluation

A third kind of feedback is useful after the speech is completed—evaluation. The simplest form of evaluation is by results. Did it work? If your goal is to be elected class president, you can judge the effectiveness of your campaign speech by the number of votes received. Of course, a loss in the election does not mean the speech was poor. Perhaps your opponent's speech was better.

Other types of evaluation are direct comments from the audience, grades, and indirect results. If you lose the race for class president but receive many compliments on your speech, you may consider the speech a success. If you are asked to represent the students at a school board meeting, you might even think the speech was very successful.

Being judged by others is part of the feedback loop. In class, teachers are constantly evaluating you by grading tests and assignments. Speeches are graded so you can tell what is and what is not effective. If we had a choice, most of us would avoid evaluation. It is one of the risks of speaking in public. The opportunity to learn is the benefit.

By far, the most significant evaluation is your own. Reviewing the speech and checking the results allows you to decide what you should do differently next time and what you should use again. This kind of feedback keeps your development and improvement as a communicator "on track."

LISTENING

"Do you hear me?" "Are you listening?" If you're like most people, you've heard these questions more than once from parents, teachers, employers, and others. If you think about it, you have undoubtedly asked these questions, either aloud or silently. The two questions sound the same, but are they?

Hearing is not *listening*. The two are related in the same way that *seeing* is related to *looking*. We see and hear a great many things in a day, but how often do we look and listen? Looking and listening require effort and concentration. You see the desk in front of you, but you do not really look at it. You hear the rush of air from the heating duct, but you do not focus your attention on the sound.

Listening requires more than being aware of a sound. Listening requires concentration and attention. You must work at it because it is a skill that can be improved through study and exercises.

ACTIVITY 3   Write two paragraphs. In the first, describe a person who is listening closely to the speaker. In the second, describe someone who is not listening to the speaker. Be as specific as you can. Include descriptions of posture, eye contact, facial expressions, and other important physical features.

Listening Levels   There are several levels of listening, but three are especially important in public speaking situations. The three types of listening correspond to the three speech purposes: (1) entertainment or enjoyment, (2) information, (3) persuasion or critical listening.

Listening for enjoyment   The easiest kind of listening, for enjoyment, requires very little from an audience. If you are listening to an entertaining after-dinner speech, you are not concentrating on the significance of the speech. You are concerned only with its ability to amuse you. You do not take notes and you may not even remember it the next day. Still, listening for enjoyment requires your attention; and since the subject and situation may not be particularly important, that attention may be hard for the speaker to get and hard for you to give.

Listening for information   When you listen to an informative speech, you are listening for information. A lecture in a history class is a good example of this type of listening. Taking notes may improve your listening because you want to remember most of the speech, say, for a test. This type of listening requires more concentration than listening for enjoyment. You try to catch certain words and phrases that hint at important details to follow.

Critical listening When you listen to a persuasive speech, you are probably listening critically. This means you are not only listening, you are also questioning and evaluating. You decide if what you are hearing is a good reason for making a particular decision. If a salesperson is trying to sell you a new stereo and promises a great warranty, you will listen critically to the explanation to see if the deal is as good as promised.

The Importance of Listening When we think about communicating, our first thoughts are about talking. After all, talking seems to be the most important thing we do as communicators. In addition, talking concerns us because it seems to require effort and risk. Statistics reveal, however, that listening occupies much more of our time than talking does.

About 45 percent of a person's time is spent listening. If you attend school six hours a day, as much as 90 percent of your time may be spent listening. Why is it we notice our speaking but fail to notice our listening? Maybe it is because we see the benefits of speaking but do not realize the benefits of listening.

In fact, listening—especially critical listening—is very important. On-the-job instructions are frequently given orally. Recalling details from speeches given in meetings may mean the difference between succeeding and failing. Even good listeners may only recall 50 percent of what they hear. Retention, the ability to remember and recall information, will diminish about 20 to 25 percent after a few days. As a listener and a speaker, these statistics tell you that you must do everything you can to aid retention, especially in speeches to inform and speeches to persuade.

TALK ABOUT IT! Form a group with five or six other students. Select one of the topics listed below and discuss your views on the topic. Each person in the group should have an opportunity to state his or her opinion. After the first person has stated an opinion, the second person must summarize the first person's ideas before stating his or her own. The third person must summarize the ideas of the first two before making a statement. This process continues with each group member until the group is back to the first speaker who must summarize all opinions except his or her own.

Topics: Math and science should be stressed more heavily in the U.S.
Employers should not have to pay minimum wage to anyone under age 18.
Movie ratings should be eliminated.
Students should be given opportunities to evaluate teachers.

The following table shows some of the things you can do, both as a listener and a speaker, to improve listening.

Listener	Speaker
1. Be prepared to listen. Make sure you are ready to hear and understand what is being said.	1. Do not begin your speech until the audience is ready to listen. Wait until their attention is focused on you.
2. Sit where you can see the speaker. You will be more likely to understand the speech.	2. Make sure you are visible to as much of the audience as possible. Establish eye contact.
3. Listen for key words and phrases. When the speaker says "In other words," you know you are going to hear an explanation.	3. Use key words and phrases. Do not be afraid to tell the audience what is important and what you are doing.
4. Concentrate on the speaker. Try not to be distracted.	4. Provide sufficient variety in your voice, physical expressions, and materials so the presentation promotes concentration.
5. Take notes.	5. Organize your presentation to make it easy for the audience to take notes.

Evaluation   Listening is not the end of the speech process. Speakers expect members of an audience to listen and react. Part of the reaction to a speech is evaluation.

Think about the times you are the audience part of the feedback loop. How do you judge others? Perhaps the best way to evaluate a speech is to pretend it is a product you are being asked to buy. If you are a consumer of the speech, just as you are a consumer of toothpaste or hamburgers, consider what there is about the product (speech) that makes it appealing or unappealing.

If you were about to buy a used car, you know you should consider many important factors: cost, mileage, appearance, condition, age, etc. What factors lead to being an intelligent consumer of public messages?

A speech may be evaluated by results alone. If you judge a speech on its results, you must determine what the intended results are and then decide if the results have been met. This seems simple, but it has one weakness. In a real public speaking situation, a speaker may try to convince you to favor one side of a controversial issue. Evaluating this type of speech by results may be useful, but you cannot decide to change your own mind based on how the speech has influenced others.

The most important question concerns the content of the speech. A speech to entertain should have sufficient content to keep the audience's attention. A speech to inform should develop a topic with new and important information. A speech to persuade must give good reasons why a listener should favor the point of view supported by the speaker.

Along with the speech's content, you must consider the ethics of the speaker. If a speech is "successful" in changing the minds of the listeners, it should do so in an ethical manner. *Ethics* is a set of beliefs about what is right and wrong. We all agree, for example, that a politician running for office should not lie to gain votes. If you are an intelligent consumer of the spoken word, you will reject speeches that contain lies or half-truths.

Often, in all types of speeches, you judge the speech by the speaker's manner of presentation. You may be impressed by a speaker's enthusiasm or moved by the wording of the message. If so, you are judging a speech by your own tastes of what is pleasant or attractive. You are making an *aesthetic* judgment.

Probably your decision to accept or reject a speech will be based on a combination of factors: effects, ethics, and aesthetics.

ACTIVITY 4   Use the following ten questions to evaluate a speech given by a classmate or by someone approved by your teacher. After answering the ten questions, write a one-paragraph summary of your evaluation.

1. What is the speech's stated purpose?

2. Does the speech have an unstated purpose, a hidden agenda? Why is the purpose unstated?

3. Does the speaker want to change your attitude or behavior?

4. Does the speech contain sufficient information to accomplish its goal?

5. Are the speaker's ideas consistent with what you already know?

6. Does the speaker's position seem reasonable?

7. Does the speaker's delivery communicate enthusiasm? sincerity?

8. Does the speech seem well prepared?

9. Is the speech organized so you can follow it?

10. Does the speech make exaggerated, unsupported claims?

While the questions in the preceding activity may be enough to evaluate most speaking situations, you must learn one more type of evaluation. As a member of a speech class, you judge and are judged so you can improve speech skills.

The teacher judges you and your classmates by comparing what you did to what you should do. You and your classmates help each other through your comments. Judging to help does not require harsh criticism. In fact, evaluations of this kind usually focus on positive aspects of a speech. When you judge others, try to remember these suggestions:

1. Be positive about the good parts of the speech.
2. Give suggestions for improvement of something that was incorrect.
3. Do not make personal comments.
4. Be fair. Every speech will not be perfect.
5. Do not judge solely on your personal opinion.
6. Let a speaker be an individual; making comparisons to others can be pointless, as well as hurtful.
7. When possible, describe what you liked or disliked in specific terms.
8. Emphasize comments about things the speaker has control over and can adjust.

SUMMARY

As a speaker, you look to the audience response as one important indication of a speech's success. To improve the chances of giving a successful speech, you must establish three feedback loops: (1) anticipatory feedback during the preparation of the speech; (2) immediate feedback during the presentation of the speech; and (3) evaluative feedback after the speech.

As a member of the audience, you will usually practice three kinds of listening: (1) listening for enjoyment; (2) listening for information; and (3) critical listening. Listening is one of the most important—and most frequently used—of all the communication skills. Both as a speaker and a member of an audience, you must be concerned with effective listening.

6

Formats of Delivery

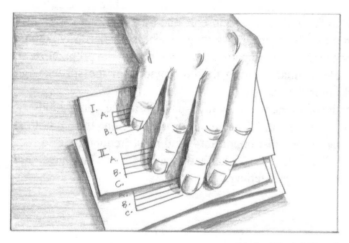

Picture This . . .

Your club has had a successful membership drive and is planning a "Welcome to the Club" banquet. The president has asked you to give a speech about the history of the club, including a review of the activities of the past year.

In preparation for your speech, you have talked to some of the older members of the club. They have told you many stories about community service projects, picnics, and fund-raising activities. You have also read all the club's newsletters—from the first to the most recent one. The only problem now facing you is how to prepare your notes so you do not forget anything. The following is a list of five methods for preparing speaking notes. Rank the methods from most to least effective. Explain your rankings.

A. Write out your speech as if it were a research report and read it.
B. Prepare an outline using a separate notecard for each category of the speech.
C. Use a combination of sentences and lists in outline form.
D. Prepare a speech, practice it several times, and then give it from memory.
E. Look at your notes the night before the speech and then give it off-the-cuff, without notes.

INTRODUCTION: Formats of Delivery

Have you ever had a conversation and, in the middle of a thought, forgotten what you were going to say? We all have memory lapses, but when a person is presenting a formal speech, memory lapses or long pauses hurt the speech's effectiveness. Audience members become uncomfortable waiting for the speaker to say something.

Good speakers present speeches that are fluent, or flow without unnecessary interruption. A fluent speech does not just happen. It takes practice from well-planned, well-organized notes.

In "Picture This . . .," you saw several options for preparing notes for your speech. Each of these represents a format or type of delivery. The four major formats are:

1. Impromptu
2. Outline

3. Manuscript
4. Memorized

Each is appropriate for some audiences, speakers, and situations but not for others.

GUIDELINES FOR EFFECTIVE DELIVERY

1. Be natural. Think of a speech as a conversation with the audience.
2. Be appropriate. Adjust the tone and formality to the audience and situation.
3. Coordinate verbal and nonverbal messages. Use voice and body to enhance and emphasize the words in your speech.
4. Reflect your personality. Don't try to imitate another speaker's style. Develop your own with the techniques that are known to produce an effective speech.
5. Be lively. Effective speakers display variety in their voices and vitality in their facial and bodily expressions.

IMPROMPTU DELIVERY

The type of delivery requiring the least preparation is *impromptu*. Impromptu delivery is not rehearsed and does not involve notes or prior planning. When a teacher calls on you in class, your response is impromptu. Even though you read the lesson being discussed, you probably did not prepare answers to possible questions the teacher would ask.

Occasionally a person will not have any advance warning or preparation before giving a speech. This often happens on special occasions, such as when a person receives an unexpected award. While impromptu speeches require the least amount of work, they are very difficult to give. An impromptu speech must be organized. It must have a clear message, even if that message is as simple as "Thank you, I appreciate your thoughtfulness." An impromptu speech should also be lively and should maintain interest. Impromptu speeches are usually brief. Audiences do not expect them to be long since there is no prior preparation. If you have watched a presidential press conference or a postgame interview with a winning coach on television, you have observed impromptu speeches.

SPEAK UP! Present a one- or two-minute impromptu speech on a topic assigned by your teacher. Topics should be similar to those on the next page.

1. What is your favorite fast food restaurant and why?

2. What would you do with a $1000 gift?

3. If you could take an expense-paid trip anywhere, where would you go and why?

4. What person has influenced you the most and why?

OUTLINE DELIVERY

One of the most common forms of delivery is from an outline. The outline includes key words and phrases that serve as reminders to the speaker. The major advantage of an outline is flexibility. A speaker can adjust the length of the speech, the number and type of examples, and the language to fit the group. By using an outline of general ideas, a speaker can address many groups from the same basic outline. Outline delivery also allows a speaker to make changes immediately before speaking. If a previous speaker said something that applies to your speech, you can make a brief note on the outline reminding you to mention the other speaker's comments. An outline can save preparation time and allow better organization than impromptu delivery.

From the perspective of delivery, the outline is not as good as impromptu or memorized delivery. A speaker must find a way to handle and look at notes without losing eye contact or eliminating gestures and movement. If a speaker is familiar with the outline and either places notes on a stand or holds small notecards, there should be fewer delivery problems.

For beginning speakers, the outline is the best method. It provides a "crutch" without tying the speaker's attention to a manuscript for every word.

Preparing an Outline An outline can be written on a set of 3x5 or 4x6 notecards or on a sheet of paper. Whichever method is used, there should be enough white space or blank areas to make it easy to see key words. White space allows for additions at the very last minute without crowding. Everything should be written large enough that it is easy to see when placed on a speaker's stand. Many professional speakers use oversized type for notes. Most word processors and printers are capable of printing a variety of font types and sizes. Select one that is bold and easily read from a distance. Most typewriters with changeable typing elements have an element for speech scripts. Compare the difference between regular type and oversized type when you are standing two feet away from this book:

Advantages of an outline

ADVANTAGES OF AN OUTLINE

While you may not have access to oversized type, you can print large letters or use all uppercase letters on a regular typewriter.

An outline can be written in words and phrases or in complete sentences. It is best to use as few complete sentences as possible. A speaker wants to glance at a few words which guide at least fifteen to thirty seconds of speaking. With the exception of the introduction and conclusion, most points should not be written in complete sentences or paragraphs. Even though introductions and conclusions should be written out, the speaker should practice them so they are partially memorized.

A speech outline using the notecard method looks something like this:

Card 1

Introduction: Everyone looks forward to Prom Night. It is a fairy tale night. We trade in our jeans, T-shirts, and running shoes for formal dresses and tuxedos. But it takes money and hard work to turn the school gym into a garden paradise. We have one year to raise money for our prom and we need to find a money-making project that will produce big profits with a minimum of time. Selling school calendars is one of the best money-making projects we could have. After I describe the calendars and how much we can earn, I think you will agree with me.

Card 2

I. Description of school calendars

    A. They are for fund-raising only

        1. Not found in stores

        2. Colorful picture for each month

        3. Over 2000 schools have sold them

Notice that the first card has the entire introduction, including the purpose statement. Card 2 outlines one part of the speech, the description of the calendars. By placing a few words on each card, a speaker can easily see all the cues. Extra notes, such as reminders to show the calendars, should also be written on the cards.

Since only a few words and phrases are on each card, a speaker should practice the speech several times. Only practice will help a speaker select and remember the explanations for each point.

Beginning speakers might want to include some complete sentences on an outline. The sentences can serve as *transitions*, which are used to connect the ideas in one part of a speech to those in another.

The following is an example of a partial outline which includes transitions. It also illustrates what an outline done on regular sheets of paper would look like.

Introduction: Everyone looks forward to prom night....
   I think you will agree with me.

I. Description of school calendars

Transition   Many of you may be thinking, "Why should we sell school calendars? What makes them so special?"
Those are two questions I want to answer. First,

A. They are for fund-raising only
   1. They are not found in stores
   2. There is a colorful picture for each month
   3. Over 2000 schools have sold them

Transition   Since you haven't seen the calendars, I've brought some samples to show you.

B. They come in three sizes
   (Show sample of each)
   1. Desk size
      a. With glossy, color pictures
      b. With space for notes

Some speakers use a colored highlighting marker to emphasize the transitions. After you have prepared and given one or two speeches, you will be able to develop a system of your own to make it easier to read your notes.

Giving a speech from an outline requires you to know how to outline. If you need to work on this skill, see pages 88–89 for a complete explanation of outlining.

ACTIVITY 1   Using one of the topics listed in SPEAK UP! write two short outlines for a speech. Prepare one version with transitions and one without.

MANUSCRIPT DELIVERY

Manuscript delivery requires a speaker to write out every word of a speech. A manuscript guarantees you will not forget what to say. It also helps you adjust to time limits. A manuscript is especially useful when you must word your comments carefully. Public figures, business leaders, and political speakers use manuscripts for several reasons:

1. They need to have a record of what they have said.
2. They need to be consistent in public statements.
3. They need to supply a copy of comments to the news media.
4. They need to select language carefully.
5. They must fill a precise amount of time.

On the surface, a manuscript is appealing to many beginning speakers. However, it is difficult to write a speech that sounds natural. Professional speech writers earn as much as $90,000 a year. They are paid that much because it is not easy to write a speech that sounds conversational.

There is a difference between public *speaking* and public *reading*. Written English and spoken English do not sound the same. To illustrate this point, read a paragraph or two from this book aloud. Now, explain the content in your own words. Is there a difference in word choice, sentence length, and style?

Written English is more formal. We do not talk in complete sentences all the time. Unless you are an experienced writer, you will have difficulty writing a natural, informal speech. There are some techniques that can help you write in a conversational style.

Preparing a Manuscript

A manuscript should begin with an outline. After completing the outline, talk through the speech. Tape-record your ideas if possible. As you begin to write, talk through each section of the speech before writing. Write what you have said. Read through the last sentence or two of what you have written and then talk through the next. Write the next section. Follow this system until the speech is completed. Then you may smooth out the rough spots and read it aloud.

Once you have finished the manuscript, you should prepare it for ease of reading. Once again, large type or writing and white space are helpful. It is also helpful to mark the script. Read through the speech and consider where you should pause or emphasize words. Underline words and use slash marks (/) to indicate pauses. One slash can indicate a short pause and two a long pause.

The following is a section from a manuscript speech. Notice the oversized letters, white space, and speaking cues. Read the speech aloud. Does it sound natural? How would you change it to make it more natural?

One morning when I sat down at the table for breakfast, /
my mother handed me the morning paper. She didn't say
anything. // She just looked at me / and then / walked back to the
stove.

On the front page of the paper was the picture of one of my
best friends // —a victim of a drunken driver.

As teenagers, / we all think we're going to live forever.
Death / is for old people. But I went to my friend's funeral. He
was only sixteen. He wasn't old, / but he was dead. //

We all like to think we are grown up enough to drink, /
even if we aren't legally old enough. The driver who killed
my friend was old enough to drink. And old enough to know
better than to drive and drink.

Since my friend's death, / I've given a lot of thought to
drinking and driving, / and I decided SOMETHING should be
done about it. I don't want myself or anyone else I know to
be the next victim. So I got involved in S.A.D.D. / —Students
Against Driving Drunk / —and I want to tell you about
S.A.D.D. in hopes you'll also get involved.

Reading a Manuscript   As you read the manuscript did you following the speaking cues? Were they natural for you? If they weren't, don't be surprised. We all speak differently, and each of us would emphasize some of the same words but not others. The main thing to remember in writing and marking a manuscript is that the speech should sound as natural as possible.

Some final suggestions regarding manuscripts concern how to read from one. There are two major delivery problems with manuscripts: reduced eye contact and unnecessary pauses to turn pages.

Even experienced speakers have to practice with a manuscript before they can have good eye contact with the audience. The President and other political speakers often solve the eye-contact problem by putting their speeches on a teleprompter. The teleprompter reflects the speech onto mirrors that look like clear glass. The speakers can see the words, but the audience cannot. The teleprompters are at eye level so the speaker does not have to look down.

Teleprompters are expensive, and few of us have access to one, but we can make adjustments in a script to improve eye contact. One technique is to write or type the speech on the top third of a sheet of paper. This will require more sheets of paper, but the speaker does not have to glance all the way down a page.

To avoid unnecessary pauses, there are two steps you can take. You can move from page to page smoothly if you have two pages of the script showing at all times. Begin the speech with page one on the left and all remaining pages on the right.

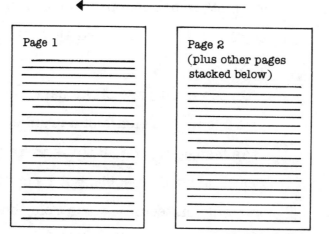

As you finish page one and begin page two, move page two to the left so both pages two and three are visible. When you are finished, all pages will be in reverse order on the left.

To make reading smoother, always end a page with a complete sentence. You do not want to switch pages in the middle of a sentence.

A final technique to help with smooth transitions from page to page is to include the last few words of one page on the top of the next page. This way, you can switch pages before you are actually at the end of the page. If you use this technique, set it up like this:

We all like to think
we are grown up enough
to drink, even if we
aren't legally old
enough.

even if we aren't legally
old enough. The driver
who killed my friend was
old enough to drink....

TALK ABOUT IT!   You will need to work with a group of four or five students for this activity. Select a speech from *Vital Speeches of the Day* or a book of collected speeches and then prepare it in manuscript form. Individually, mark the manuscript as you would deliver it. Compare your choices of emphasis and pauses. Each student should read sections of the speech. Is the speech written in a conversational style? Rewrite the sections that are not conversational.

SPEAK UP!   Using one of the topics in SPEAK UP! on page 39, prepare a manuscript speech and present it to a group of students. Have group members comment on your conversational style, use of pauses, and emphasis.

MEMORIZED DELIVERY

The final format is memorized delivery. This is the most difficult delivery to use, because you must prepare a manuscript and then memorize it.

Memorized delivery is the common format in speech contests. It is also used by many professional speakers. Often, professional speakers prepare a general speech on a topic with broad appeal, such as motivation or how to be successful. They give the same speech to audiences across the country, with little or no adaptation. Much of the speech's appeal is in the delivery. By memorizing the speech, the speaker can give full attention to movement, gestures, and appealing vocal delivery.

Often a memorized speech sounds and looks more like a dramatic performance than a conversational talk. If the original manuscript is written in a conversational style, the memorized speech will sound conversational. Depending on the purpose and audience, a dramatic approach can be appropriate. When a speaker's purpose is to entertain, a well-rehearsed, memorized speech produces the best comic timing.

Speakers using a memorized format also encounter problems with physical delivery. What do they do with their hands since there are no notes to hold? Should they move about since there is no reason to stand behind a podium? Many students address these problems by planning their gestures and movements; however, too often planned movements look planned. They can distract more than help. Work on memorization and vocal delivery and let gestures flow naturally.

One important point to remember when giving a memorized speech is that audience members are not following along with a copy. If you do not say something exactly as it was written, no one will know.

Perhaps the biggest disadvantage to a manuscript speech is that it is inflexible. If an audience looks confused, you cannot add another example easily.

HANDLING QUESTION AND ANSWER PERIODS

Often a speech is followed by a period in which the audience can ask the speaker questions. Prepare for this period ahead of time by anticipating all possible questions. Ask yourself what areas are complex or have potential for disagreement. Think about the answers you would give. Practice them.

When answering a question, repeat the question first. This gives you additional time to formulate your thoughts and ensures that everyone knows what question you are answering. Make eye contact with all audience members, not just the questioner, during the answer. Try to relate your answer to all members of the audience, not just to the questioner.

Refer back to your speech in giving answers and elaborate on what was said. Show understanding for those with disagreements, but reemphasize your position. Do not be critical of someone who disagrees.

Announce when you are ready to take the last question. Briefly summarize the major point of your speech and new information revealed during the question and answer period, and thank the audience before leaving the podium.

SUMMARY

Good delivery begins with the selection of a delivery format which best suits the speaker, audience, and situation. In most cases, a speaker has prior warning that he or she will give a speech. There are three delivery formats a speaker can select for speeches prepared ahead of time: outline, manuscript, and memorized. When a speaker has no advance notice, the speech format used is impromptu.

Each delivery format has advantages and disadvantages. A speaker should weigh each before selecting a format. Beginning speakers are advised to use the outline format.

Speakers should learn the appropriate methods for dealing with questions.

All speeches, regardless of format, should be organized, should have clear beginning and ending points, and should be fluent. Practice is essential for success; even the impromptu speaker must have experience to perform well.

7

The Voice

Picture This . . .

One of your friends is running for a class office. The campaign has been very exciting, and you suspect that the election will be very close.

On the day before the voting, each candidate will give a speech. The auditorium will have a microphone and loudspeaker. The speech will be given to about 300 people.

Before the speech your friend asks you for advice. She feels she has some problems in preparing. First, she is not originally from your state, and she worries that her accent will bother the audience. Second, she has never used a microphone before, and she worries about using it incorrectly. Third, she only has three minutes to give her speech, but the first draft of her speech takes at least four minutes unless she talks rapidly.

What is the *best* advice you can give your friend? What is the *worst*? Explain.

A. Try to speak without the accent.
B. Speak naturally; the accent won't really bother the audience.
C. Speak rapidly to get the four minutes of material within the time limit.
D. Cut the amount of material to suit the time limit.
E. Practice with the microphone so there won't be so much worry.
F. Rehearse the speech at home.
G. Do nothing. Everything will work out fine. Too much worrying will hurt the speech.

INTRODUCTION: The Voice

A trademark is a very important part of any business. Individuals and companies spend hundreds of thousands of dollars establishing and protecting their trademarks. Makers of soft drinks, automobiles, and other consumer products recognize the need for a unique, identifiable symbol of their goods. In an important way, your voice is also a trademark.

In "Picture This...," your friend obviously understood the importance of good vocal delivery. We can recognize literally hundreds of voices. We associate these voices with actors, politicians, television and movie characters, and broadcasters. Usually a "trademark" voice is very different in one or more ways from a "normal" voice. Bill Clinton's voice, for example, is known for its frequent hoarseness and Southern accent. Actor Robin Williams is known for the energy and variety in his voice. Arnold Schwarzenegger's trademarks are his deep voice and Austrian accent.

Whether you know it or not, your voice is your trademark. It may not be known beyond your own group of friends, but it is associated with you and your ideas. Like a major corporation, you can control your trademark to some extent. By thinking about your voice and its effect on others, you can develop an appealing and clear vocal style.

TALK ABOUT IT!   List ten famous speaking voices of people either living or dead. Make sure you use voices that almost anyone would recognize. Divide into groups of three or four and share your list with your group. Combine the lists to form a class list of the ten most identifiable speaking voices. In your group, try to get as many of your own choices as possible on the group list.

YOU ARE IN CONTROL

As a student you probably feel that many areas of your life are controlled by others. Teachers, parents, school administrators, and others control much of your behavior. But when it comes to using your voice, *you* are in control. You have the power to control your voice so that it serves your purposes.

To understand the control you have over your voice, think about how you adjust a television set. You must use several controls to get the kind of picture you want. Each control changes a variable. For example, the contrast control changes the difference between light and dark. The brightness control alters the amount of light from the screen, and so on. Each time you change a control, the picture changes quality.

Your voice is equipped with a set of controls, too. The three basic controls you can adjust are *volume*, *rate*, and *pitch*. By learning to manipulate these controls, you can make your voice very expressive. Almost without thinking, you can communicate anger, disappointment, sorrow, excitement, and countless other emotions. You can even say one word in many different ways.

If you can already use volume, rate, and pitch, why study it? Unfortunately, speaking in public is not always as easy as talking casually with a friend. When you stand in front of a group, the natural liveliness and expression in your voice may be lost. This can harm a speech, since *variety* in volume, rate, and pitch is an important part of keeping the audience attentive and open to your ideas. Without variety, your voice becomes flat and monotonous. You can compare vocal variety to variety in the things you eat. Most of us like pizza, but the thought of eating pizza for every meal is unpleasant. Our need for variety makes us eat other things. An audience's need for variety in voice makes it important that you use all the natural expressiveness that makes your conversations lively and interesting.

Volume

The first control we worry about is *volume*—that is, how loud and soft your voice is. This is the first concern because without good volume, no one in the audience can hear you, no matter how good your speech might be. The word *audible* means "able to be heard." Above all, your speech should be audible.

If you are sure your speech is audible, you can begin work on variety in volume. By using your volume control, you can emphasize certain words, phrases, or passages of a speech. Imagine that you are giving a speech about a very exciting concert you attended. Your speech may be soft as you tell about buying the tickets, finding your seat, and waiting for the show. But can you imagine using a very quiet, calm voice to describe the climax of the concert with a laser light show, smoke bombs, and other special effects? Again, the key is variety. If you use a loud voice throughout the speech, the audience cannot tell from the volume when you are really excited.

TALK ABOUT IT!

Variety in volume is even important within a single sentence. By emphasizing, or "punching," one or two words within a sentence, you can make the sentence mean different things. Divide into groups. Read these sentences aloud and then talk about how punching the italicized word changes the meaning.

1. *I* saw the game.
2. I *saw* the game.
3. I saw *the* game.
4. I saw the *game*.

5. The *photographer* took my picture.
6. The photographer *took* my picture.
7. The photographer took *my* picture.
8. The photographer took my *picture*.

Emphasizing a word by increasing volume can be particularly helpful when you use key words in your speech. Think about the volume usually used to deliver Lincoln's famous phrase "*of* the people, *by* the people, and *for* the people." Or consider Franklin Roosevelt's famous line ". . . the *only* thing we have to *fear* is *fear* itself." Without "punch" these lines lose some of their impact.

Volume is important even within a word. English words of two or more syllables will emphasize at least one syllable. The word *table* requires you to punch the first syllable. Try saying *table* with the accent on the wrong syllable. It does not even sound like an English word. Some words (*record*, for example) change meaning with a change in emphasis.

Rate

Speed is a synonym for *rate*. The speed at which you speak helps communicate your ideas to an audience. A rapid rate may communicate anger, excitement, or impatience. A slow rate might show fatigue, hopelessness, caution, or some other mood or emotion.

When you are at ease, the rate of speech usually takes care of itself. When you are nervous, however, you may begin to speak rapidly without even knowing it. Many people have prepared what they thought was a five-minute speech, only to find that it lasted three minutes in front of an audience! A rapid rate can also cause problems with articulation and pronunciation. When you speak too rapidly, it is easy to skip a syllable or emphasize the wrong syllable.

ACTIVITY 1   The English poet Robert Browning wrote a version of the Pied Piper. Early in the poem he describes a town overrun by rats. Read the stanza to yourself. Read it aloud twice, the first time reading it slowly and deliberately and the second, reading it rapidly. Write a paragraph answering the following questions: How does the speed change the stanza's effect? How does your mental image of the rat-infested city change? How did the rapid rate affect your articulation?

> Rats!
> They fought the dogs and killed the cats,
>   And bit the babies in the cradles,
> And ate the cheeses out of the vats,
>   And licked the soup from the cooks' own ladles,
> Split open the kegs of salted sprats,
> Made nests inside men's Sunday hats,
> And even spoiled the women's chats
>   By drowning their speaking
>   With shrieking and squeaking
> In fifty different sharps and flats.

Too rapid a rate can also damage one of the speaker's most important tools—the pause. An old proverb states, "The greatest wisdom is knowing when to remain silent." The silences that a speaker uses between words and sentences add drama and meaning to a speech. You have probably heard speakers who know precisely when and how long to pause to set up a word or phrase.

ACTIVITY 2   During World War II, Winston Churchill's radio speeches aroused Britain and helped generate the spirit needed to cope with great problems. Copy the following passage from Churchill's wartime radio addresses. Read them through, and then mark the pauses. Use one slash (/) for a short pause and two slashes (//) for a long one. (Punctuation has been removed.)

"I have nothing to offer but blood toil tears and sweat."

"You ask What is our aim I can answer in one word Victory victory at all costs victory in spite of all terror victory however long and hard the road may be for without victory there is no survival."

"Let us therefore brace ourselves to our duties and so bear ourselves that if the British Empire and its Commonwealth last for a thousand years men will say 'This was their finest hour.' "

One particularly effective use of the pause is called *framing*. By pausing slightly before and after a word or phrase, you can frame it and give it added emphasis. Read these sentences without framing.

"Have you ever read one of Poe's short stories? It may be scary even to you."

Now read the sentences again, but frame the phrase "even to you." Do you notice the difference? The framing gives the sentences drama—and even a bit of playfulness.

ACTIVITY 3   In each of the following sentences at least one word or phrase can be framed effectively. Write down the word or phrase, and then check your answers with your classmates. How does different framing create different meaning? (Punctuation has been removed from within the sentences.)

1. Too many students lack one important characteristic of successful salesmen confidence.

2. The jeweler said he would put the bracelet aside for me for a slight fee.

3. You might call America's hockey team an underdog since no player was over the age of twenty.

4. What do we mean by this word leadership?

5. To a real student this assignment offers many challenges.

Pitch   Nowhere is being in control more necessary than in pitch. *Pitch* is the word used to describe the highness or lowness of your voice. You can think of it as notes on a musical scale. Just as a melody takes you up and down a musical scale, speaking requires you to use varieties of pitch to express your meaning.

You learn to use pitch very early in life. Even small children know that a question requires a rise in pitch at the end. The sentence "Have a nice day" may be a question or a statement, depending on how you use pitch on the word *day*.

Naturally, your pitch is determined in part by the range of your speaking voice. If your voice is quite low, you seek variety within the range you naturally use. Likewise, if your voice is high, you would be foolish to try to speak using low pitch. You must find a range that suits you.

Within your natural range, you establish patterns for the changes in pitch. These patterns are called *inflection*. Some actors are so skilled that a one-syllable word like *me* or *no* can be inflected using many different pitches.

ACTIVITY 4   Pronounce the words in the list, altering your pitch to reflect the meaning indicated in parentheses.

1. Me (Are you talking to me?)   4. Four dollars (Is that all?)

2. Me (I didn't do it.)   5. Four dollars (That's what it costs.)

3. Me (I'll do it.)   6. Four dollars (not five)

If these seem easy, use the sentence "I love you" as your model. How many ways can you say it? Write a word or phrase in parentheses that describes the meaning of each inflection you try.

Practicing Voice Controls   Understanding that you can control volume, rate, and pitch is not much use unless you plan to use them. The best way to develop variety is to rehearse your speech aloud. Frequently, students will go over a speech "in their heads," never saying the words until the speech is given. If you rehearse aloud, however, you will hear what the audience hears. You can say a phrase several ways to find out how you want it to sound. If you can test your speech on a friend, do so. Your friend may offer suggestions that you have not thought of.

Another method of planning the controls is to mark a script. Sometimes you can use a manuscript to your advantage if you underline words you want to punch, identify pauses, or note inflection for rehearsal.

Impromptu speeches rely heavily on natural vocal variety *and experience.* Whatever type of speech you want to give, plan to use the control you have over volume, rate, and pitch.

SPEAK UP!   Find a brief (2½ to 5 minutes) poem or story. Copy it down leaving a space between each line. After you have familiarized yourself with the poem, go through your script and mark it for meaning. Place slashes (/) where you plan to pause. Underline words and phrases that need increased volume. Write brackets around framed words. Draw parentheses around words or passages that need decreased volume.

Now rehearse the reading aloud. Give the reading in front of the class. Make sure you have a brief introduction, telling the title and author of your reading.

CLARITY

Even if you control variety, you may not get your message across unless your vocal presentation is clear. You may think a clear voice is something a person is born with. While it is true that some people seem to have voices that are more appealing than others, there is still much you can do to give your voice clarity.

Pronunciation   The first thing you should do to improve clarity is pronounce words correctly. Most of the time you have no trouble pronouncing words. In normal conversation you choose from a fairly limited set of familiar words. Because a speech may require using a broader word choice, you may have to use words that are less familiar. Also, an audience in a formal speaking situation may be less tolerant of mispronunciation than a friend might be.

If you are going to use unfamiliar words, make sure you check their pronunciation. How do other people pronounce them? How does the dictionary show the pronunciation? Even with these aids, you may mispronounce some words simply because you never learned the correct pronunciation. Review the list of some commonly mispronounced words. Think of how you have heard them pronounced. If you are unsure about the correct pronunciation, look up the words.

Often	Cavalry	Picture
Secretary	Ninety	Athlete
Library	Preferable	Drama
Probably	Formerly	Statistic
Arctic	Yesterday	Lengths

Make sure the key words in a speech are pronounced correctly. A mispronounced key word can be confusing, unintentionally humorous, and embarrassing. For example, a student giving a science report on nuclear energy should be careful not to say "nuculer," the common mispronunciation.

One thing more needs to be noted about pronunciation. The area in which you live may determine how you pronounce words. If your manner of speech is common to a region or group within the country, you probably are speaking one of the many dialects of American English. A dialect may have its own vocabulary and its own grammatical rules, as well as its own pronunciation. Usually people love to hear a dialect. Midwesterners are usually charmed by New Yorkers, and vice versa. A Southern accent is often regarded as a distinct benefit in some kinds of public speaking. Whatever accent you have, it is part of your trademark. As long as it is clear and appealing, an accent should probably be left alone.

Enunciation

Even if you pronounce your words correctly, your vocal clarity may suffer from poor *enunciation*. In other words, you are not forming your sounds clearly and distinctly. When you speak in small groups with people who are familiar with your speech pattern, enunciation may not be a problem. In large groups and with an audience less familiar with your voice, good enunciation is essential.

Many enunciation problems stem from lazy habits. Your tongue and lips, since you can control them, must be used to form clear, accurate sounds. Lazy use of tongue and lips leads to mumbled, muffled sounds that may be barely intelligible to an audience.

Other enunciation problems result from speed. If your rate of delivery is too fast, you may find yourself slurring words and phrases. Your tongue, teeth, and lips are falling behind in your "speed race!" Listen to yourself, taking others into consideration. Watch their reactions to your speaking and listen to their comments.

TALK ABOUT IT!

One entertaining means of becoming more aware of correct enunciation is to try to read and write words as they are often said. In groups, "translate" the following list of muffled, slurred sentences into standard written English and then read each one aloud.

1. Jeetyet?

2. Idoe wanna go.

3. Whudja halfer breakfuss smornin?

4. Hazzeol papern the cornera thyard been pitup?

5. Jillunme are gonna star the car bar selves.

Now write your own slurred, muffled sentences. See if your classmates can translate them. Make sure you "giddum right."

One of the oldest and most enjoyable ways of practicing articulation is to say tongue twisters. You probably know many yourself, but try these before challenging the class with your own. Remember to start slowly and build speed—and make sure your enunciation is clear.

- Rubber baby buggy bumpers.
- Shall she sell sea shells?
- Toyboat. (Repeat several times, building speed.)
- Ten tiny trumpeters tunefully tooting their ten tiny trumpets.
- She thrust three thousand thistles through the thick of her thumb.

SUMMARY

You can control your voice by changing volume, rate, and pitch. These three controls contribute to effective speaking, both formal and informal. At the same time, your effectiveness as a speaker is helped or hindered by how you pronounce words and enunciate them.

As always, the audience is the ultimate test for vocal delivery. Ask yourself these questions:

- Was my speech loud enough to be heard?
- Did I vary my volume to express emotion, emphasis, etc.?
- Did I vary my rate to suit the meaning of the speech?
- Did I use pauses effectively?
- Did I frame important words?
- Did my voice vary in pitch, or was it monotonous?
- Did I know how to pronounce all the words?
- Were the words enunciated clearly?
- Was my delivery natural?
- Did I mark my manuscript?
- Did I rehearse aloud?

You may use this checklist to make the most of your vocal delivery and establish your own vocal trademark.

8

Nonverbal Delivery

Picture This . . .

Imagine that you are very tired. You were up late last night studying for a test. Now you are experiencing a letdown after taking the test. Your next class is about to begin, and you are going to listen to two guest speakers. The two speakers are very different in their approaches.

Speaker A begins with a humorous story. She moves around in front of the class and gestures naturally and frequently. She shows a great deal of emotion in her face. Her voice changes in volume and pitch and she varies her rate of speaking. In addition to explaining her topic verbally, she has prepared several charts. She uses no notes, so she looks directly at the audience throughout the speech.

Speaker B has a prepared speech. He seldom looks up from his notes. He stands behind the podium during the entire presentation and holds his notes. His voice has some variety, but there is very little change in his facial expressions.

When evaluating a speaker's effectiveness, which of the following do you consider important? Explain your choices.

A. Knowledge of the subject matter
B. Eye contact with the audience
C. Liveliness of movement and delivery
D. Speaking loud enough to be heard
E. A pleasant voice
F. A well-groomed, confident appearance

INTRODUCTION: Nonverbal Delivery

Good delivery requires more than a good spoken presentation. Effective delivery also includes nonverbal delivery which complements the verbal delivery. Research has shown that we tend to learn more when we receive information through more than one channel or method. Each of the five senses can be considered a channel of communication. When you listen to a speech, you are also watching the speaker. Thus, you receive information through two channels—hearing and seeing. You have learned about the characteristics of vocal delivery, and now you will learn about six nonverbal characteristics that make a speech more interesting:

1. Posture and stance
2. Movement
3. Gestures

4. Eye contact
5. Facial expressions
6. Appearance

In addition to these elements of bodily delivery, you will learn how to use visual aids in a speech. Visual aids are a nonverbal delivery technique that can add life and variety to your presentation.

POSTURE AND STANCE

The way you stand has a great deal to do with how you sound as well as how you move. Unless you have erect posture, it will be difficult for you to breathe properly. Without adequate breath control, your verbal delivery will be affected. You will not be able to project your voice as well, and you will have to take more breaths which will make your delivery choppy.

Erect posture also communicates that you are interested in your topic and are serious about giving the speech. Someone who slumps over the speaker's stand or shifts from one foot to another can appear disinterested or nervous. Try to stand with both feet firmly planted. Distribute your weight evenly on both feet. Do not stand with your feet parallel (Figure 1). This will allow you to rock back and forth or to sway. Your feet should be spread slightly apart and should be placed so that you can move easily throughout the speech (Figure 2). The diagrams show two ways of placing your feet. Clearly, the stance in Figure 2 will give you better balance and will prevent distracting movement.

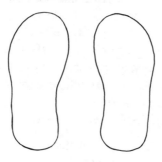

Figure 1. Standing this way makes it easy to sway or rock. Avoid this stance if possible.

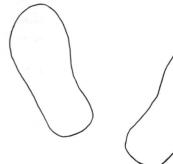

Figure 2. This stance gives you a firmer footing. It is also easy to move from this position.

MOVEMENT

Most of us think that speakers stand behind a podium and never leave that spot. Recall some of the speakers who captured and held your attention. Did they move? They probably did.

Movement says several things to an audience. First, it says that a speaker is moving to a new point of discussion. Second, it helps the speaker get closer to the audience. This makes the audience feel as though the speaker is really communicating to them. Third, it keeps the audience from getting bored. When a speaker moves, audience members must shift their focus. This keeps them alert. Finally, movement uses up some of the speaker's nervous energy and is a positive way to release natural tensions.

While movement can help a speaker emphasize a point or get closer to an audience, it is possible to move too much. A speaker does not want to pace or move unnecessarily; such movement often communicates nervousness. When a speaker is nervous, the audience can begin to feel restless and uneasy.

Movement should be natural. Do not plan when you are going to move. Often when speakers program their movements, the movement is not matched with the words and the movement looks awkward. Use movement to emphasize your ideas but only if it complements your delivery.

ACTIVITY 1 Write a short paragraph describing the person's stance, movement, or walk in one of these situations:

- A football player walking off the field after a defeat
- A comedian presenting a routine on a television show
- A person who has waited in line for over an hour to purchase tickets
- A young child waiting for her parent to finish talking on the phone to a friend

Write the paragraph as if you were describing a character in a short story or book.

GESTURES

Most beginning speakers worry about what to do with their hands. Usually we are not even aware that we have hands when we talk; but when we are standing in front of a roomful of people, our hands and arms seem larger than life.

The use of hands can be a real asset to a speech. Gestures add emphasis and help us describe. Speakers who are exciting to watch use many emphatic gestures, such as stabbing the air with a finger or pounding the podium. These gestures show that a speaker is excited and involved in the content. A speaker who wants us to visualize something can use gestures to help us create images.

The best advice regarding gestures is to let them develop naturally. If you select a topic you are truly interested in and if you practice your speech, gestures will come easily. Think about your speech, not about your hands. As you become more experienced, it will be easier to gesture without giving it much thought. To free your hands so you can gesture, avoid grasping the sides of the podium or holding your notes with both hands. Many beginning speakers do both. Remember, movement of any kind uses energy that comes from anxiety about giving a speech. If you can release that energy through gestures and movement, you will give a better speech.

EYE CONTACT

We all like to have the feeling that a speaker is actually talking to us alone. In our culture, we tend to think a person is more trustworthy if that person looks us in the eye. A speaker who looks down through most of a speech not only loses our attention but also loses our belief and trust.

The key to having good eye contact is knowing your material. Practice in impromptu delivery increases your skill in establishing eye contact with the audience. Practice will also help you know your material and rely less on your notes.

Eye contact helps the audience feel part of the speech, and it also helps the speaker. Audience members give clues to their interest, understanding of the topic, or agreement with the content. Speakers who watch the audience receive valuable feedback, which helps them adjust the speech when necessary. If a speaker notices that audience members are straining to hear or see, then the speaker can adjust the delivery by speaking more loudly or moving closer.

Eye contact should be directed to all parts of the audience. It is easy to find one or two friendly faces and to look at no one else. However, all audience members need to be addressed. This does not mean that you must move your head constantly. In fact, you can switch eye contact with only a slight movement of the head. If you practice your speech in front of friends or family members, have them sit apart. This will force you to look in more than one direction.

FACIAL EXPRESSIONS

Our faces communicate a great deal about us. Turn off the volume on a television set and watch the actors' faces. Often you can tell what their moods are and what attitude they are conveying. Look around any classroom and you can tell which students are interested, bored, tired, or daydreaming.

A good storyteller uses more than his or her voice to read or tell a story. Facial expressions also communicate the story. As with gestures, facial expressions should be natural. This aspect of nonverbal delivery is the one over which you have the least control and know the least about. The best way to determine if you have a lively face is to videotape a speech and watch yourself. If you are interested and involved in your topic, your face will communicate that to the audience.

ACTIVITY 2   If you have never played charades, your teacher will explain the rules. Using movie, song, or book titles, give clues to your classmates through facial expressions, gestures, and movement only. No talking!

APPEARANCE

While it is not necessary for you to dress up to give a speech in class, you should be aware that your appearance can add to or detract from your message. If you are wearing a T-shirt with a cute picture or saying, your audience may pay more attention to the shirt than to the message.

Your clothes should be neat and should not distract the audience in any way. Avoid wearing jewelry that you can play with unconsciously. Also avoid wearing caps or other accessories that might draw attention from the speech.

When giving a speech in a setting other than the classroom, choose your clothes to fit the occasion. Obviously, if you are speaking at a formal dinner, you should wear a suit or dress, not blue jeans and a T-shirt. Your appearance can communicate a great deal about you and about your attitude toward the event you are attending. Part of occasion analysis should include learning what is the appropriate dress for the occasion.

VISUAL AIDS

In addition to the nonverbal delivery you create with your body, you can use the visual channel by including visual aids in your speech. Several visual aids are commonly used in speeches:

1. Chalkboard
2. Posters
   a. With charts or graphs
   b. With words or phrases
   c. With drawings
3. Objects or models
4. Audiovisual equipment
   a. Transparencies on an overhead projector
   b. Pictures on an opaque projector
   c. Slides
   d. Films
   e. Videotapes
5. Handouts
6. Yourself

Whatever visual aid you select, be sure it *supplements* the speech rather than becomes the speech. There can always be too much of a good thing. Each of the visual aids listed can be used properly or improperly. We will now discuss the correct usage for each.

Chalkboard The chalkboard is the easiest visual aid to use. You do not have to prepare anything ahead of time or bring something to class. When using a chalkboard, keep the following in mind:

1. Write large enough so everyone can see. Print instead of write—it is usually easier to read.
2. Do not write too low on the board. People in the back of the room cannot see the bottom of the chalkboard.
3. Stand on one side of what is written. Do not block the board. Use a pointer if necessary.
4. Do not speak with your back to the audience while you write on the board. Write first and then speak. If possible, put your notes on the board before your speech and then pull a screen or map over them. You do not want anyone to read your notes before you are ready to explain them.

Posters Many speakers prepare their visual aids ahead of time by placing them on large pieces of poster board or newsprint. Professional speakers often have easels that hold large tablets of newsprint. A speaker can write on several sheets of the tablet and then turn to one page at a time. When preparing posters, use the following guidelines:

1. Use dark ink—black, blue, and red are best. Yellow, pink, and light green are difficult to see from a distance.
2. Write in clear, large letters.

3. Put one idea on each sheet. Do not clutter the page. Remember, you want the audience to focus on one idea at a time.
4. Tape the poster to the chalkboard or place it on the chalk tray. Holding the poster restricts your ability to move and hides you from the audience.
5. Only show the poster when you are ready to discuss it and remove it as soon as you have described it.

When to use posters
Posters can be used to preview or summarize your main ideas. For example, in an informative speech on swimming, you might want to present the four main swimming strokes. So in the beginning of your speech, you uncover your first poster and point to the words *freestyle*, *breaststroke*, *butterfly*, and *backstroke*. Your audience now knows what to expect in your speech. When you are ready to review the main points, you simply return to the first poster.

Posters, especially with drawings or pictures, are helpful when you want the audience to have a complete, exact picture of what you are describing. In the speech on swimming, for instance, drawings of a swimmer doing each step of the backstroke would complement your description of the steps.

Graphs
When you are presenting statistical information, it is helpful for the audience to see and hear the numbers. This is especially true if you use several statistics. Graphs are one of the best means of explaining statistics, especially when you are comparing statistics. Following are three types of graphs: pie, line, and bar.

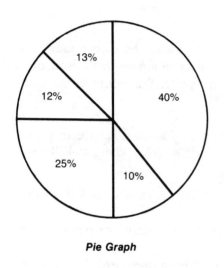

Pie Graph

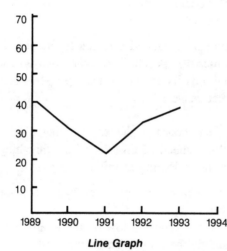

Line Graph

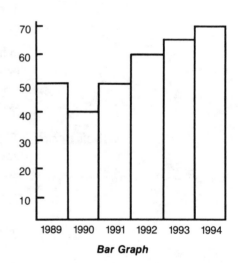

Bar Graph

ACTIVITY 3
Describe the kind of poster you would use to illustrate the following:

1. An explanation of how a club's dues were spent: 20% on the newsletter, 40% on the club trip, 35% on community service projects, and 5% on miscellaneous expenses.

2. A description of the parts of a ten-speed bike.

3. An example of the changes in the number of students enrolled in computer courses from 1980 to the present.

4. A summary of the important food groups.

Explain why you selected each kind of poster.

Objects or Models   Often you can show an actual object or model as part of your explanations. Typically, objects and models are used in demonstration speeches. At the conclusion of this lesson, you will be given an assignment for a demonstration speech. As part of that speech you will want to use at least one of the visual aids you have learned about.

When using an object or model, be sure it is large enough for everyone to see. Likewise, be sure to place it on a desk or hold it up so everyone can see it. Remember not to obstruct the view by the way you stand.

Audiovisual Equipment   A more professional means of presenting material is with audiovisual equipment. Slides, movies, transparencies, videotapes, and pictures shown with an opaque projector—all can add a great deal to your speech. There are several things to remember if you use any mechanical or electrical equipment. First, be sure you have extension cords and that you know where the outlets are. You might need to rearrange a room if the electrical outlet is not located in the proper place.

Second, be sure you know how to use the equipment. No one wants to sit through several silent minutes while you try to figure out how to focus an overhead projector.

Third, be sure the equipment is in good working condition before you begin the speech. Always test the equipment before class begins.

Fourth, have extra light bulbs or marking pens (for overheads). There seems to be a rule when using equipment that if a light bulb is ready to burn out or a pen to go dry, it will do it in the middle of your speech.

Overhead Projectors   Business, professional, and educational speakers often use overhead projectors to supplement their speeches. An overhead projector casts an image from a piece of transparent plastic onto a screen. Many of the same hints that help with chalkboards can help with overheads. Overhead projectors have several advantages:

- A speaker can use an overhead—even write on it—without turning away from the audience.
- Because overhead projectors enlarge writing, larger audiences can benefit from the projections.
- Overheads can be prepared ahead of time. Speakers don't have to write while they speak.
- Overheads can be photocopied to include pictures and graphs.
- Overheads can be used again and again.

You can make your speech more interesting by using overheads, but you'll need to remember several hints:

1. While you prepare your overheads, be sure they are prepared with care. Check that spelling is correct. Check to be sure that ideas are expressed clearly.
2. Limit the amount of information on each transparency. Some speakers make the mistake of giving the audience far too much to read. The transparency should support your speech, not distract from it.
3. Keep your transparencies in order. Many speakers use transparencies to organize their speeches, but if the transparencies are out of order, a speech can become confusing. Many speakers number their transparencies.
4. Check your transparencies on the overhead projector before you speak. This helps you determine if your audience will be able to see them well.
5. Transparencies that will be used many times can be mounted for easy handling.

6. Remember: cover part of a transparency if it is going to detract from your speech. For example, if the top part of your transparency asks a question, you can cover the answer on the bottom half with a piece of paper.

Slides   Business and professional speakers also use slides to enhance a speech. Slides can be expensive, but they are essential in some speeches requiring vivid visual examples—speeches about medicine, art, architecture, and many other topics. If you use 35mm slides, you may take them yourself, check them out from a library, or create them on special computer programs. Charts and diagrams can be represented in high clarity and full focus. Unlike overheads, however, slides require a room to be almost completely dark. If your audience will be uncomfortable, lose attention, or be unable to take notes, perhaps slides are not a good choice. Much of the advice for using overhead transparencies can be applied to slides as well. Remember: slide projectors require you to advance slides, usually with a remote control. Practice your speech with the slides and a slide projector. Practice will help you anticipate problems.

Handouts   Rather than prepare one poster or chart for everyone to see, many speakers prepare drawings or charts on regular typing paper and make copies for everyone to follow. There are some benefits to doing this, but there are also hazards. A speaker always risks losing the audience's attention while distributing the handouts. There is also no guarantee that audience members will stop looking at them when you are ready to move on to something else.

To avoid some of the problems, do not hand out the material until you are ready to explain it, and have someone help you distribute it to reduce time.

It is not a good idea to pass single copies of material or objects around the class during the speech. This tends to create a distraction. If you have an object that is too small for everyone to see, then you should reconsider using it and think about using a drawing instead.

Yourself   You can be a visual aid. Many topics allow you to demonstrate something to the audience. The following sample demonstration speech requires the speaker to be a visual aid in order to demonstrate relaxation exercises. For instance, if you were to demonstrate the proper way to hold a tennis racket for a serve, a forehand shot, and a backhand, you would be part of a demonstration.

If you are part of the visual presentation, remember the rules for all other visuals. Be sure everyone can see you. Be sure your movements are "large" enough for everyone to see what you are doing. And try to demonstrate more than once to guarantee everyone understands. Unlike a picture or poster, what you do is seen for only a short period of time.

SAMPLE DEMONSTRATION SPEECH

The demonstration speech that follows explains how to do something and shows the audience how to do it. Notes in the margin show you what the speaker did during the speech. Imagine being in the audience. Do you think it could be an effective speech?

How to Break from Study before Study Breaks You
by Sue River

How many of you have found yourselves studying late at night with a final exam facing you in the morning? Your neck is stiff, your back hurts, your head aches, and your eyeballs feel ready to fall out of their sockets. I've had that experience, and today I'd like to talk with you about a way to break from study before study breaks you. I will demonstrate some simple exercises you can do in just a few minutes to help release some of this built-up tension in your body. These exercises will help you return to your studies refreshed and ready to study more effectively.

The exercises I will show you can be done in five minutes, but they will have a long-lasting effect. Instead of taking a break to get some coffee, a soft drink, or something to eat, you can take a break that will benefit you four ways.

First, exercise relieves physical and emotional tensions that build up while studying. Everyone is nervous before taking a test or while working on a paper. When tensions are eased, you will perform better.

Second, exercise replenishes your vitality and energy. Think about the last time you still had twenty pages of a history chapter to read and you couldn't keep your eyes open. If you had only taken a few minutes to get the blood circulating again, you would have been able to read those twenty pages and then some.

The third reason for taking an exercise break is that it clears your mind. We all are guilty of cramming before "the big exam," and things tend to get mixed up. A break will give you an opportunity to unclutter your mind before you add new information to it.

The last reason for taking a break is that you will return to your work refreshed and will make better use of your time. By taking out five minutes, you will use the next thirty more productively.

As I said already, all these benefits can be yours with some simple exercises and five minutes of your time. I want to demonstrate four exercises for you: the spine stretcher, the neck saver, the back stretcher, and the eye exerciser.

The spine stretcher helps relieve tension in your elbows and shoulders. It releases energy locked into your spine and it brings blood into your head for your eyes and brain.

To do this exercise, stand with your hands clasped behind your back. Keep your feet a few inches apart. Breathe out and slowly bend as far down as you can go comfortably while bringing the arms up. Hold for a count of five. Slowly come up. Repeat.

Now that you have your shoulders loosened, move up to your neck. That is where a great deal of tension is centered. The neck saver and the back stretcher are designed to relieve tension in your neck, head, and back.

The neck saver is done by placing your chin on your chest. Roll your head slowly and evenly in a continuous circle all the way around until you have circled it from your right shoulder to your back, to your left shoulder, and back to the chest again. Rotate your head five times to the right and five times to the left.

After completing the neck saver, you want to do the back stretcher. For this exercise, you don't even have to get out of your chair. If you have room, you might try doing this one along with me. Sit toward the edge of your chair with your legs extended outward straight in front of you with your heels on the floor. Bend forward and hold your upper calves firmly. Bend your elbows outward and very slowly and gently pull your trunk down. Relax all muscles, including those of your neck, so that your head hangs

Specific speech purpose

The speaker showed a chart with the four benefits listed.

The speaker moved away from the podium so everyone could see her.

The speaker paused briefly while the audience made room to do the exercise.

down. Hold without motion for a count of ten. Very slowly straighten up and rest a moment. Now reach forward and down farther, as far as the lower calves or the ankles, if possible. Go through the same motions and hold for a count of ten. Slowly straighten up and rest.

You should be feeling much better, but there is one last part of your body you shouldn't ignore—your eyes. This last exercise, the eye exerciser, helps remove tension from your eyes. If you wear contact lenses, don't do this one with them in place. It is also a good idea to remove your eyeglasses. This is one all of you without contacts should be able to do along with me. Begin by widening your eye sockets and holding them wide throughout this exercise. Move your eyes slowly to the top of the sockets. Hold for one second in that position. Slowly roll your eyes to the extreme left. Move them slowly and make the muscles work. Keep the sockets wide at all times. Hold for one second. Remember, this is not a continuous rolling of the eyes. You should hold each position. Now roll your eyes slowly to the extreme bottom. Keep the sockets wide. This wide position helps to remove tension in the muscles around the eyes. Hold for one second. Slowly roll your eyes to the extreme right. Hold for one second. Repeat this routine of the four positions and perform ten times in all. The eyes should move slowly and rhythmically and you must feel that the muscles are getting a workout by moving to the extreme positions in the sockets.

Now close your eyes and place your palms over them. Hold for a minimum count of 30. Turn your mind inward and attempt to hold it "thoughtless" for this brief interval.

Those of you who followed along with me should be ready to go to your next class refreshed. Remember, the best way to relieve tension, to replenish your energy, to clear your mind, and to make the most of your study time is to take an exercise break. The exercises I have shown you take only a few minutes, and you can do them anytime, anywhere.

Studying isn't fun and it isn't easy, but by following the procedures outlined in this handout I will give all of you, you can learn how to break from study before study breaks you.

The speaker distributed handouts at the conclusion of her speech.

SPEAK UP!   You are to give a three- to five-minute demonstration speech. A demonstration speech explains how to do something by actually showing an audience how to do it. If you ever watched a cooking show on television or seen a lab demonstration by a science teacher, you have watched a demonstration speech. There are several guidelines to follow in selecting a topic for a demonstration speech:

1. Select a topic that can be demonstrated easily in the classroom. It is not possible to show how to water ski in a classroom, but it is possible to demonstrate how to swing a bat or dribble a basketball.
2. Select a topic that can be demonstrated in the time allotted. Very few things can be demonstrated completely in three to five minutes; however, you can narrow your speech to cover one aspect of a topic.
3. Prepare part of the demonstration ahead of time. You can show all stages of a process by preparing parts of each stage in advance. For instance, if you show how to refinish a piece of furniture, you should have one part of it with old finish to show the removal stage, another part with the finish already off, another with the sanding done, another with primer, and another with the new finish on.

4. If you need someone to assist you, ask the person ahead of time and prepare him or her for the part.

5. Talk as you demonstrate. Try to avoid long silences.

6. Be sure everyone can see what you are doing. Repeat if necessary, perhaps standing in different parts of the room. You may have to ask audience members to move to the front of the room.

The complete assignment criteria are explained on the evaluation form included in this lesson. Read the sample demonstration speech for an idea of how to present such a speech.

SUMMARY

Giving a speech requires more than talking. There is a visual, or nonverbal, element to speech delivery. How you stand will help with your vocal delivery as well as provide you with a solid footing to move without being awkward.

Movement can indicate transition points in a speech and can help you get closer to the audience. Gestures can provide emphasis and description. Eye contact helps your listeners feel that you are speaking to them, and it allows you to watch audience members for valuable feedback.

Facial expressions complement your vocal delivery and add life to your speech. Your appearance can indicate that you are serious about speaking. You should not distract attention from what you are saying to what you are wearing.

In addition to what you do with your body to assist audience members in understanding your speech content, you can prepare visual aids to clarify ideas. Visual aids should be used to supplement your speech; they should not become the entire substance of the speech. You should practice using visual aids until you are comfortable with them and use them effectively. If audience members cannot see your posters, all of your hard work will be for nothing. Practice, preparation, and common sense will make using visuals more effective in your speeches.

Evaluator _____

Demonstration Speech

Name _____

Instructions: Each category will be rated on a scale of 1–5: 1-poor, 2-fair, 3-good, 4-very good, 5-excellent. Within each category, individual requirements are to be rated with a + or −.

I. SPECIFIC ASSIGNMENT CRITERIA   1 2 3 4 5

_____ Speech met the 3- to 5-minute time limit.

_____ Speech met criteria for a demonstration speech.

_____ Visual aid was used.

_____ Speech was presented in outline form.

II. ANALYSIS   1 2 3 4 5

_____ Speaker adhered to general and specific speech purposes.

_____ Speech was narrow enough to be fully developed and handled adequately in time allotted.

_____ Topic was appropriate for demonstration development.

_____ Topic was appropriate for the audience.

III. SUPPORTING MATERIALS   1 2 3 4 5

_____ Visual aids were appropriate.

_____ Visual aids were used correctly.

_____ Speech utilized sufficient clarifying materials (i.e., examples, illustrations, etc.).

IV. ORGANIZATION   1 2 3 4 5

Introduction was properly developed:

_____ Gained audience attention and created interest.

_____ Oriented audience to the speech.

_____ Included a clear and precise thesis statement.

_____ Major ideas were forecast.

_____ Organization of the speech was clear and easy to follow.

_____ Transitions provided necessary links between ideas.

_____ Speech utilized appropriate signposts and internal summaries.

Conclusion was developed properly:

_____ Summarized the speech content.

_____ Provided a link back to introductory comments.

_____ Provided an idea for the audience to remember.

V. DELIVERY TECHNIQUES   1 2 3 4 5

_____ Stance and posture were appropriate.

_____ Eye contact was appropriate.

_____ Facial expressions helped to convey/clarify ideas.

_____ Gestures added emphasis and description.

Vocal delivery was effective:

_____ Appropriate volume   _____ Appropriate rate

_____ Conversational style   _____ Enthusiastic

_____ Clear enunciation   _____ Uses pauses correctly

_____ Vocal variety   _____ Fluent delivery

VI. WORD USAGE/LANGUAGE   1 2 3 4 5

_____ Language was direct and made the speaker's point clearly.

_____ Words were used appropriately.

_____ Grammar was appropriate.

_____ Word pronunciations were correct.

_____ Language was suitable for the audience.

COMMENTS AND SUGGESTIONS FOR IMPROVEMENT: TOTAL SCORE _____

9

Style

Picture This . . .

You are being considered for a job. The pay is quite good and the work is something you really want to do. The job requires you to meet the public as a representative of the firm for which you want to work. You have gone through one preliminary interview, and two other people are being considered along with you.

Each of the three has been invited to an interview with the three people who will make the hiring decision. You are asked to prepare a five-minute presentation on your background and qualifications. The letter you received stressed that the hiring committee is very interested in knowing more about you than might be read on a job application. Because you will meet the public in this job, the company wants to be sure you have communication skills in addition to a good school and work record.

As you prepare your presentation, you try to present yourself and your personality. What can you do to show your personality?

A. Carefully choose your language. The words and phrases you choose say more about your personality than anything else.
B. Carefully select the clothes you plan to wear. The way you dress will probably have greater effect than what you say.
C. Make no special plans. A spontaneous presentation will be most effective.
D. Keep your words and phrases simple. Use a normal, everyday vocabulary.
E. Make a point to use words which show your knowledge about language and communication.
F. Try to set a light, humorous tone.
G. Try to set a serious tone.

INTRODUCTION: Style

Each time you make a speech, you present more than information and ideas. You present yourself. As you know already, presenting yourself is often the most important part of speaking. When you have seen other students make speeches, you have probably thought, "I would do it differently" or "I would never say that" or "I could never do something that way." Those responses are natural. It is expected that no two people will do things exactly alike. As you probably noticed when discussing "Picture This. . .," different students would use different approaches to the presentation, depending on how they view themselves, the job, and the interviewing committee. It all comes down to one important thing: style. We all have different styles because we have different personalities and because our speeches serve different purposes with different audiences.

LETTING YOU COME THROUGH

Whenever you speak or write, you are presenting yourself to others. In a way, choosing how to say something is like getting dressed. As you decide what to wear, you probably consider many factors. What is the weather like? Where will I be going during the day? What will be comfortable? Who will I be likely to meet? How do I feel today?

Choosing words requires similar considerations. You must consider the situation, the occasion, the audience, as well as your own feelings and goals.

Definitions *Style* is the *way* something is said or done, rather than *what* is said or done. Sometimes people act as if style does not matter. They say, "What difference does it make how something is said as long as it gets said?" Even a very brief consideration of famous sayings shows that the way something is said is important. When Abraham Lincoln began the Gettysburg Address, he could have said "Eighty-seven years ago. . ." instead of "Four score and seven years ago. . ." Which is more memorable? Thomas Jefferson could have ended the Declaration of Independence with "We are totally committed." Instead he said, "We pledge our lives, our fortunes, and our sacred honor." That phrase went down in history.

What's the difference? Why does one speech live on in the memories of an audience and another fail to keep an audience's attention for five minutes? The answer is style. The goals of style are clarity, grace, and economy. *Clarity* means stating your ideas in a clear, understandable manner.

Unclear: Calling a new client on a telephone which is a real problem is made easier by the new telephone system.

Clear: Calling a new client on the telephone has been a real problem. The new telephone system makes it easier.

Grace means stating your ideas in a pleasant, skillful manner.

Awkward: Helping the network's ratings will not result from the new television shows this season.

Graceful: This season's new television shows will not help the network's ratings.

Economy means stating your ideas as briefly as you can without sacrificing clarity or grace.

Wordy: In today's modern society, the students of high school age must add additional courses to their schedules if they are going to be fully prepared in a complete way for a successful career.

Economical: Modern high school students must take more courses to prepare for a successful career.

Good style is achieved through hard work and experience. The tools you use to create your style are word choice, word arrangement, and figures of speech.

WORD CHOICE

If you want someone to stop talking, you may say any of the following: shhh; hush; shut up; be quiet; quiet; stop talking. Each conveys the same meaning, but each also conveys much more. Your own attitude is expressed by your word choice. Depending on the situation, some of the words may not even be appropriate or fitting.

Levels of Usage   Good word choice may differ from situation to situation. One difference you need to be aware of is the difference between writing and speaking. First, your writing vocabulary is probably larger than your speaking vocabulary. Casual conversation may draw on only a few hundred common words, but writing usually requires more. Second, writing follows stricter rules of grammar than speaking. For example, sentence fragments are not acceptable in writing, but they may be used effectively in speaking.

You must also decide if the situation requires formal or informal word choice. In a pep talk during halftime, a coach will use less formal language than he or she might during an awards ceremony at the end of the season. If your audience expects formality, you will have to respond with formal word choice. If not, you may need to rely on common, familiar words. When Lincoln dedicated the cemetery at Gettysburg, the formal occasion made ''Four score and seven'' appropriate. When you are asked to empty the trash, you probably would not say, ''Wait three score seconds'' instead of ''Just a minute.''

ACTIVITY 1   Many formal words have an informal synonym. Write an informal synonym for the words in list A and a formal synonym for list B. You may use a dictionary or thesaurus.

A

- The concession stand sells many *beverages*.
- At noon we took an *intermission* for lunch.
- The movie was interrupted by *paid commercial advertisements*.
- Her boss passed around a *memorandum* on using the new office machines.
- This new product will *sanitize* the kitchen floor in just seconds.

B

- Linda went to work for the new *car* dealer.
- Leroy's new employer went *broke* last month.
- The old cabin was full of *bugs*.
- My *boss* checks my work each night.
- The minister told the *kid* to wait for her father.

Since speech is less formal than writing, it is easy to fall into the habit of using slang. *Slang* is language that obeys very few of the standard rules of formal language. Slang is common in many very informal situations. Often it is colorful and expressive. (One author called slang, language which ''takes off its coat, spits on its hands, and goes to work.'') Slang is seldom appropriate in a speech, however. There are several reasons.

---

1. Some slang is offensive, especially outside its informal situation. Some audiences will be uncomfortable with slang.
2. Many assume that a person who uses slang does so because he or she does not know how to use more formal, dignified language.
3. Slang changes quickly. If you use slang, you are never sure if the audience understands it or if the meanings you intend are outdated.
4. Frequently slang will appeal only to a group of people who are just like you. Slang may not be understood by people who are younger, older, wealthier, poorer, etc.

TALK ABOUT IT!   Divide into groups. Write sentences containing current slang that might be confusing to an older audience. Rewrite the sentences by substituting more understandable language.

Appropriate word choice, like almost everything else, comes down to finding the best means to communicate your ideas to a particular audience. The words you use in conversations with your friends differ from the words you use in making a report. Consideration of your own purpose and the audience's needs determine appropriateness of word choice.

Effective Word Choice: Exactness   One of the most troublesome problems in preparing a speech is finding the exact words to communicate an idea. Because our conversations are full of very general, almost meaningless words, we sometimes use them in speeches. Words like *stuff* and *things* are so general that no one knows what they mean. If a friend says he's got ''some stuff to do,'' what do you know? Hardly anything. If he says, ''I have some errands to run,'' you know more because the word *errands* expresses more than the word *stuff*. If he says, ''I have to pick up my aunt's plane tickets and run them over to her apartment,'' you know precisely what he will do.

Audiences appreciate specific, concrete word choice. Concrete words are accurate and precise. A *concrete* word will give the audience an image that helps communicate exactly what you mean. *Abstract* words are the opposite. They are not precise. They give no vivid mental picture. For example, if a friend walks in the room and says, ''Something funny just happened in the hall,'' you are not sure what she means. *Funny* could mean hilarious, puzzling, unusual, amusing, or shocking—all of which are more concrete words than *funny*. Even more concrete would be a description of what your friend saw: ''I just saw two students wheeling Mr. Chambers down the hall on a library cart.''

ACTIVITY 3   Words have various degrees of concreteness and abstractness. Write down each word below, and then write one word that is more concrete and one word that is more abstract. For example, considering the term *sports car*, a more abstract word could be *automobile* and a more concrete word could be *Corvette*.

Show   TV drama   Lost   food   Dessert   ice cream   Sport

Jewelry   ~~Sing~~   Rock star   Slash   Novel

Guitarist

Sometimes making a speech more concrete is as simple as answering the six basic questions: Who? What? When? Where? Why? How? Rather than complain that "Some people have done some things to upset students," you could say, "The committee decided yesterday not to allow people to bring their dates to the party" and "This decision has angered many people who have already planned on bringing dates." By asking the questions as you prepare the speech, you do not leave unanswered questions for your audience to worry about.

Another means of increasing the concreteness of your speech is to emphasize sense impressions. Try to give your audience specific ideas of how things look, smell, taste, feel, and sound. When you can, describe a person, place, thing, idea, or event so the audience can imagine exactly what you have in mind.

ACTIVITY 4   The following paragraph is full of words that are very abstract. First, identify those words, then rewrite the paragraph so it is more concrete. Remember to use specific words and ask the questions: Who? What? When? Where? Why? How?

I like summer days. They're really neat. I think the sunlight is nice. It makes me feel good. There are so many things to do on a summer day that I have trouble deciding. Of course, a lot of stuff to do depends on nice weather. It's kind of weird when I plan something and it rains. It makes me feel bad. But the next time the sun shines, I forget all about the bad times and try to enjoy the day.

Jargon   Another common problem in word choice is the use of jargon. *Jargon* is language that is made up of the specialized, technical words of a specific job, hobby, or social group. If you are a person who knows a great deal about computers, you probably know many words that others do not—words like *bit*, *byte*, *user-friendly*, *floppy disk*, *dot matrix*, etc. If you use those terms when you speak to an audience, will they know what you mean? If they do not, what have you accomplished? Probably nothing except angering or boring a group of people you wanted to entertain, inform, or persuade.

Triteness   Jargon hurts understanding because it is unfamiliar to an audience, but some language is *too* familiar. In other words, it is used so often it has become *trite*. Trite language lacks freshness and originality. People have heard it so much that they either ignore it or dislike it. Worn out comparisons such as "cool as a cucumber" or "solid as a rock" are trite. Trite expressions are easy to use because you really do not have to think about them.

FIGURES OF SPEECH

In literature, a figure of speech allows a writer to say one thing and mean another. If a poet states, "The vacant eyes of the building stared down the street," we know the poet is writing about the building's windows. In speaking, the term *figure of speech* has a broader meaning. It simply is a name for extending language beyond its normal use. There are two kinds of figures of speech. The first is based on word order; the second is based on word meaning.

Word Order   The English language uses word order to create meaning. ''The dog bit the man'' means something entirely different from ''The man bit the dog.'' Changing ''The band is ready to play'' to ''Is the band ready to play'' makes a question out of a statement. Because it is so important, word order can be used to improve style in many ways.

Balance in words and phrases   When a sentence or a paragraph is arranged so words and phrases seem to go with each other in length and structure, we say they are balanced. Balance is natural, since language usually follows a set of rules you have known since you were small. For example, you would never say, ''I practice dancing and to play basketball.'' You would say the balanced sentence, ''I practice dancing and playing basketball.'' *Dancing* and *playing* balance.

Parallel structure. The previous example illustrates parallel structure. This means that words that are logically related (*dancing* and *playing*) are stated in similar ways (both have an *-ing* ending). Within a sentence, you should be on the lookout for opportunities to use parallel structure. Audiences like it because it sounds right to them. You can probably hear the problem and its correction in this example:

Incorrect: A carpenter must learn to read blueprints, about understanding geometry, and how to use surveyor's tools.

Correct: A carpenter must learn to read blueprints, to understand geometry, and to use surveyor's tools.

Do you *hear* the difference? When you rehearse, talking aloud will help you find and use parallel structure.

Antithesis. Antithesis is like parallel structure except that opposites must be paired together. Notice the neat and balanced sound to these examples.

''Let us never negotiate out of fear, but let us never fear to negotiate.'' (John F. Kennedy's Inaugural Address)

''Not that I loved Caesar less, but that I loved Rome more.'' (Brutus explaining why he murdered Caesar)

''The world is a comedy to those who feel and a tragedy to those who think.'' (Horace Walpole)

REPETITION

One of the easiest and most effective uses of word order is repetition. This simply means repeating a word, phrase, idea, or even a sound. This technique is so popular that a glance through any newspaper or magazine will show plenty of repetition. A convertible's top is ''air-tight, noise-tight, and moisture-tight.'' A brand of shoes claims to be ''a shoe so soft even Mother Nature approves.'' A makeup ad promises ''longer, richer, lovelier lashes.''

1. Repeated Sounds. *Alliteration* is the repetition of consonant sounds. *Assonance* is the repetition of vowel sounds. Both can be used to make a speech appealing.

''We were numbed by the nightmare of nuclear war.''

''Try as I might, I could not lie to the person who had trusted me.''

2. Repeated words. Often a repeated word sounds awkward. A planned repetition, however, can be stylish.

<u>We</u> <u>shall</u> go on to the end, <u>we</u> <u>shall</u> <u>fight</u> in France, <u>we</u> <u>shall</u> <u>fight</u> on the seas and oceans, <u>we</u> <u>shall</u> <u>fight</u> with <u>growing</u> confidence and <u>growing</u> strength in the area, <u>we</u> <u>shall</u> defend our island. . . <u>we</u> shall <u>fight</u> on the beaches, <u>we</u> <u>shall</u> <u>fight</u> on the landing grounds, <u>we</u> <u>shall</u> <u>fight</u> in the fields and in the streets, <u>we</u> <u>shall</u> <u>fight</u> in the hills; <u>we</u> <u>shall</u> never surrender . . .
(Winston Churchill)

By listening to yourself and trying to hear the speech as your audience might, you can improve your style by experimenting with word order.

ACTIVITY 5   Label the kind of word arrangement used in each sentence: parallel structure, antithesis, alliteration, or repeated words.

———— 1. Math was Lewis Carroll's hobby. Math was his love. Math was his door to fantasy.

———— 2. Give a man a fish and he will eat for a day, but teach him to fish and he will eat for a lifetime.

———— 3. Our natural body rhythm is a clock that counts the seconds, measures the minutes, and determines the days for our intellect and emotion.

———— 4. A new mascot for the school would increase student enthusiasm, build fan support, and guarantee a more successful athletic program.

———— 5. Everyone knows what needs to be done, but no one wants to do it.

Now write a paragraph in which you use at least three of the techniques described in this section.

WORD MEANING

Changing a word's meaning does not mean changing it altogether. It means using a word in a new and exciting way. You are already familiar with many of these stylistic changes because you have read and studied them in literature classes.

1. Metaphor and simile. Both metaphors and similes are comparisons between two unlike things. A simile uses the words *like* or *as* to make a comparison. A metaphor does not.

"After our last science field trip, some of us came back looking like scarecrows." (simile)

"The question of enforcing requirements was a hot potato that the committee passed around." (metaphor)

2. Irony. Irony occurs when you use a word but intend it to mean the opposite of its normal meaning.

"Burying the money in the back yard before the flood came was a *great* idea."

"I'm sure that all of you *love* to take tests on nice, spring days."

3. Exaggeration. When you say something that everyone knows is exaggerated, you often call attention to your point. This technique is also called *hyperbole*.

"They'll never get the idea in a million years."

"My car was so dirty that the automatic car wash spit it out."

4. Understatement. When you intentionally say less than you mean, you do the opposite of hyperbole. Still, you call attention to your point.

"Only a handful of people really understand nuclear power."

"The Olympic Games were watched by a few people."

5. Rhetorical question. When you ask a question during a speech but expect no answer, you are asking a rhetorical question. A rhetorical question is another way of making a statement or of getting your audience to think.

"Have you ever stopped to think how many U.S. coins are in circulation at this very moment?"

"Have Americans forgotten the meaning of the word *freedom*? My answer is 'No!' "

SPEAK UP!   Now that you have studied some of the elements of style, you should put them to work. Someone described a pet peeve as "that thing you love to hate." Select a pet peeve from the list below or provide your own. Write a manuscript speech making use of the ideas in this lesson. Remember to use everything you have learned about delivering a manuscript speech. Focus on using appropriate language, effective word choice, and figures of speech.

Topics

TV ads	Kinds of clothing	Pets
Sports broadcasters	A brother or sister	Going to the dentist
Video games	Eating in a restaurant	Going to the doctor
Kinds of food	Being alone	Homework
Nervous habits	Big dogs	A particular entertainer
Diets	Little dogs	People's voices
Phone calls	Nosy people	Your boss
The weather	Cooking	Cars
Interruptions	Girls	Makeup
Other drivers	Boys	Long trips

TONE

The final consideration in this lesson is tone. Each time you choose a word, you are displaying your attitude toward your subject. As the author of the speech, you establish tone. In a speech on driving, for example, you might take a humorous approach. Your word choice would probably establish a light tone. Perhaps you choose to warn your audience about traffic hazards in your community. If so, your tone will probably be concerned. If you are saying the community should spend money to correct the hazards, your tone might even be one of outrage. These various attitudes will be disclosed in part by the sound of your voice and your nonverbal communications, but word choice will also be important.

SUMMARY

Style in speaking depends on many things, but word selection is one of the most important. You must make a speech your own by displaying your own attitudes and personality. Good style achieves the goals of clarity, grace, and economy. By choosing words that are appropriate and specific, you may present an idea in a manner that is acceptable to your audience. By avoiding jargon and triteness, you maintain clarity and appeal. Figures of speech further your style by allowing language to do more work than it might do in ordinary conversation. Do not forget: each word is important. The tone of your speech is greatly influenced by word choice.

10

Research

Picture This...

As part of the requirements for your physical education class, you must give an oral report. Part of the assignment requires you to turn in a list of the sources you used in preparing your report. The teacher has a list of topics that students must select from. You were absent on the day of selection, and the teacher assigned you the history and growth of women's sports in America.

Since you know very little about the subject, you will need many sources of information. You have only two class periods for library work; the report is due in one week. Since you do not have much time, you must schedule your work very carefully. Which of the following materials would you use? Which do you think would not be very useful?

A. Library books on sports
B. Library books on women's rights
C. Recent magazines
D. Encyclopedia articles
E. Almanacs
F. Biographies on famous women athletes

INTRODUCTION: Research

When we speak to an audience, we prefer to talk about things we already know about. Our experience, hobbies, jobs, and opinions are fairly easy to talk about since the material for the speech comes from within us. Like a store clerk, we simply take inventory of the information we already hold in our memories.

Nevertheless, we are often required to speak on topics that are new to us or for which we need new information. In classes like English, American history, government, and science, students are frequently assigned topics so they can learn new things and share them with others. Even when you can choose your topic, you often cannot find a topic on which you are an authority.

If you wonder why using research materials is so important, think about giving a speech on women and sports. You probably do not know much, so you need to get information from somewhere or from someone. Even if you know a little about women athletes, you have to convince your listeners that your speech is correct. You can "borrow" the authority you lack by referring to famous, well-qualified people who write about the subject. After all, your audience would be likely to believe information from the president of the National Collegiate Athletic Association.

Even outside the classroom, researched speeches are necessary. In community life, a citizen may want to speak out about tax increases. A speech with facts, figures, and quoted opinions will convince more people than the general statement that "taxes are too high already." In business and industry, too, a researched speech is frequently needed. If a new law has been passed that changes working conditions, someone has to research the law and present it to the people it affects. If a new product is being purchased—for hundreds, thousands, or millions of dollars—many well-researched presentations must be made. Often the best researcher proves to be the most effective speaker.

A quick survey of speech purposes reveals the importance of using resource books and resource people. In a speech to entertain, you may need to find interesting facts, clever sayings, humorous anecdotes, or funny stories. Do you have all these things stored in your memory? An informative speech must present new information to an audience. Do you always have new information on any topic ready to present in an interesting manner? A persuasive speech must change people's minds. Can you recall the kind of convincing, authoritative information that will cause people to think seriously about your position? Even if you have a fine memory, the answer to these questions is probably no. We all need help from outside sources.

THE LIBRARY/MEDIA CENTER

When you think of research, you probably think first of the library or media center. One writer called it the memory of civilization, for it contains the greatest thoughts of men and women since the invention of writing. Almost any subject, unless it has come to light only in the past few days, can be researched in a library. Libraries serve a very useful function—they remember so we do not have to. Considering that tens of thousands of books are published in English each year, it is good that someone keeps track, files, and stores for us.

Books Books in a library are usually broken down into two categories: fiction and nonfiction. (A library may have separate sections for paperbacks, short stories, or other groups; but even these will be fiction or nonfiction.) *Fiction* is the product of an author's imagination; therefore, fiction is not used for research unless you are looking into the works of a particular author. *Nonfiction* books are the backbone of library research. That is not to say that everything in the books is necessarily true. Nonfiction books deal with subjects in a factual way, without benefit of characters and plots created by the author.

Dewey Decimal System Most high school, college, and public libraries organize their nonfiction books by the Dewey decimal system. The word *decimal* means "ten." The ten divisions of the system are easy to learn. This list tells you the numbers designated for each division.

000-099	General works	500-599	Pure Science
100-199	Philosophy	600-699	Useful arts
200-299	Religion	700-799	Fine Arts
300-399	Social Sciences	800-899	Literature
400-499	Language	900-999	History

Each of these ten divisions is assigned ten subdivisions. Each subdivision has ten more divisions. A book may then be classified and shelved by one Dewey number. For example, cookbooks will probably be in the 600s (where home economics is classified), in the 640s (the division assigned to home economics and cooking). The number 641 will probably refer to a few specific cookbooks. Books can even have decimal points (641.2) and the author's initials (641.2/CR).

The Library of Congress System Another way of organizing resources in the library or media center is the Library of Congress System. Rather than use numbers to label the primary categories, the Library of Congress System uses letters. Instead of ten categories, the system starts with twenty. A typical entry looks like this:

LN
504.2
P

Here are the twenty categories in the Library of Congress System:

A	General Works	N	Fine Arts
B	Philosophy, Religion, Psychology	P	Language and Literature
C	History—Auxiliary Sciences	Q	Science
D	History—except America	R	Medicine
E-F	America	S	Agriculture, Plants, and Animal Husbandry
G	Geography, Anthropology, Sports		
H	Social Sciences	T	Technology
J	Political Sciences	U	Military Sciences
K	Law	V	Naval Sciences
L	Education	Z	Bibliography, Libraries, Library Science
M	Music		

When you find a book, your research has just begun. If you are going to speak on lasers, you find a book on lasers. Do you have time to read the whole thing? Probably not. If you have narrowed your speech, your subject may be something like "the medical use of lasers." You can then use the book's index and table of contents to find the material on the medical use of lasers. Browsing through the book may be interesting, but using indexes and tables of contents saves time.

Card Catalog What is the key that opens the Dewey system up to you? The card catalog. The card catalog is really a huge index of the whole library. It is constantly changed to show accurately the library's holdings. Each book may appear many times, depending on the subjects it deals with. Every book will have three cards at least: an author card, a title card, and a subject card.

The three cards are the same except for the first line. If you know an author who has written about your subjects, you can find all the books by that author in your library. If you know the title of a specific book, you can find it quickly. Since you probably do not know this information, your most useful card is the subject card.

Books may be indexed by more than one subject to make finding specific books easier. When you find your subject, it will appear in bold print at the top of the card. Beneath it will be information about the book. Most important, the Dewey call number will be in the upper left corner. This number guides you to the part of the library and the specific shelf where this book is stored. Remember that if your sources are not under the first subject you look up, try again. "Fishing" may be listed under "water sports." "ESP" may be found under "para-psychology."

Today many libraries use computers to store information on their books. Although the information appears on a screen rather than on an index card, the information itself is the same. Books can be located through author, subject, or title. In addition, computer systems often tell users if the book they want is in the library or if it has been checked out. Every library computer system has careful instructions on how to use it, and usually help is available from librarians who will show you how to use the computer catalog.

Many school and public libraries also offer research services available through a computer hook-up. Sometimes the information may be on a compact disc (CD-ROM), as in the case of an encyclopedia or other reference book. With the help of a librarian or media center specialist, you can even go "on-line" and use a database. On-line research can get you to the most up-to-date sources quickly. Each on-line service requires only basic research skills, but you may need the help of someone familiar with the service, the database, and the computer commands to get started.

ACTIVITY 1 Use the following subject card to answer the five questions below. Write out your answers.

② GHOSTS AND SPIRITS

138.87   Carver, Andrea. ③

C   ④ Things that go bump in the night: great

①   unsolved ghost mysteries. Cummings and

⑤ Kissel, Inc (1980). ⑥

156p. ⑦

⑧   A re-telling of the ghost stories that
have been investigated and reported on by
scientists throughout the world.

⑨   1. Parapsychology I. Title

1. Call number
2. Subject heading
3. Author of book
4. Title of book
5. Publisher

6. Copyright date
7. Number of pages
8. Annotation (summary of contents)
9. Headings of other cards in the catalog

1. Who is the author of the book?

2. What is the book's call number?

3. When was the book published?

4. How long is the book?

5. What is the book's title?

Reference Books A reference book is a special book containing specific information that can be found easily. Usually reference books may not be checked out of the library and are set apart in a special room. These books are the most efficient sources of information in the library. It takes little time to find a great deal of information. Encyclopedias, dictionaries, almanacs, and yearbooks are examples of reference books.

Periodicals Magazines, the most commonly used library periodicals, are essential to effective research. They contain the most recent information, they cover the broadest range of topics, and they are relatively inexpensive to obtain. Almost any speech can use information from a magazine article. Even if your speech is on Greek history, magazine articles are still being published about that subject. Often the magazine title is little indication of the magazine content. Experience and questioning the librarian is the best way to determine which magazines are suitable for your purpose. This list gives the title and a brief description of content of only some of the many magazines in a library:

Newsweek (general current events)
Time (general current events)
U.S. News and World Report (current events, specifically politics, business, economics, and social issues)
Congressional Digest (issues currently confronting Congress)
Sports Illustrated (current events in sports)
Atlantic Monthly (politics, social issues, the arts)
Current History (foreign affairs, politics)
New Yorker (current events, the arts)
American Heritage (American history and culture)
Vital Speeches (politics, business, social issues)
The Nation (politics and social issues)

The *Readers' Guide to Periodical Literature*

Finding a single magazine article may sound very difficult, but because of the *Readers' Guide to Periodical Literature* it is quite easy. The *Readers' Guide* directs you to magazine articles on specific subjects. It is arranged in alphabetical order by subject. While each library may have its own method of getting the magazine you want, *Readers' Guide* can tell you which magazine to ask for.

If your subject is animation and you narrowed the topic to computer animation, you may begin by looking up "Cartoons." You soon find that the correct entry to search is "Motion pictures—animated cartoons." Under this subject you may see several entries. This one is typical.

New computer animation fools the eye. N.
  Shapiro. il Pop Mech 156:76-7+ Ag 81

The entries are quite easy to read.

1. Title of magazine article: *New computer animation fools the eye*. The title is given first. Only the first letter is capitalized.
2. Author: *N. Shapiro*. The author's name is second.
3. Special features: *il*. If the article contains illustrations (il) or portraits (pors), the entry will tell you.
4. Name of magazine: *Pop Mech*. The title of the magazine is usually abbreviated. All abbreviations are listed at the front of each *Readers' Guide*.
5. Volume and page numbers; *156:76-7+*. On the left of the colon, the volume number is listed. In some libraries you must know the volume number to get the magazine. On the right of the colon, you will find the page numbers of the article. If you forget to note the page numbers, you may waste time searching for the article once you have the magazine.
6. Date: *Ag 81*. The date of the magazine is abbreviated. For weeklies, the complete date is given (Ag 7 81). This, too, is essential in requesting a magazine.

ACTIVITY 2

Study the following entry done in the style used in the *Readers' Guide*. Write your answers to the seven questions by using the information in the entry.

Making the grade in back-to-school fashions.
  P. Rambow. il New Youth 17:7-12 S 5 84

1. What is the title of the magazine article?

2. Who wrote the article?

3. Does the article contain any special features? If so, what?

4. What magazine is the article in?

5. What volume of the magazine is the article in?

6. What are the page numbers for the article?

7. What issue (date) of the magazine contains the article?

Other Resources
In addition to the familiar sources, libraries can provide many other opportunities. It is a mistake to think that libraries only contain books and magazines. Most modern libraries are really media centers, because they branch out into film, recordings, CDs, pictures, videotapes, and more.

Audiovisual materials
If your library contains films, you may be able to use them for research. More likely, filmstrips and slide kits are available. Using these resources and the scripts that often come with them, you can frequently find important information as well as visual aids. More and more, libraries offer videotapes for their users. Most audiovisual (AV) materials are indexed in the card catalog, so they are easy to find.

Pamphlet file
The pamphlet file (also called the vertical file) is a collection of pamphlets, leaflets, reprints, and clippings. The library staff files them according to subject so people can have easy access to them. A pamphlet file can contain many items unavailable anywhere else: a government reprint, a clipping from the local paper, or copies of the leaflets passed out in a public campaign. These, too, are frequently indexed in the card catalog. However, it may be worthwhile to check the entire file on a subject you are researching.

Biographical sources
Often students choose to speak on a famous person. If you have decided to talk about someone on whom no complete book has been written, you may use one of the other biographical resources. Some provide very brief information (*Who's Who* and *Who Was Who*). Others provide information on only one kind of person (*Contemporary Authors*, or the Kunitz-Haycroft author series). *Current Biography* is one of the most useful of the biographical sources. It provides biographical information, a picture, further references, and the famous person's mailing address. The mailing address is useful if you want to write about further information. Add these resources to the reference books mentioned earlier and to the various biographical encyclopedias on scientists, women, politicians, sports figures, rock musicians, etc., and the library can provide materials for speeches on almost anyone.

PEOPLE AS RESOURCES

Often library materials are not enough. You may choose to interview someone who has special knowledge about your subject. Many people in your community can give you information on such subjects as recent history, careers, hobbies, local community issues, school concerns, local history, and many others. A speech on the Great Depression of the 1930s, for example, will probably be more interesting if you can interview someone who lived through it. Not only can you get more information for your speech, but also you can make your subject seem more immediate to your audience.

Interviewing takes time, courtesy, and work. Remember the following rules for a good interview:

1. Make an appointment. "Dropping in" on someone can be rude. Moreover, if your resource person has time to prepare, you may be treated to special pictures, displays, or stories.
2. Be ready. A person who grants an interview is doing you a favor. Show up with a list of questions. Know the subject of your speech. Read an encyclopedia article or a magazine clipping. Going into the interview "cold" can waste your resource person's time and your own.
3. Take notes. Be sure that you record information accurately and completely. If you want to tape-record the interview, ask permission at the time you make an appointment. Many people do not like the idea of speaking while being taped.
4. Be courteous. By being punctual, appreciative, and grateful, you can make your interview go much easier. Courtesy should always be extended.

TALK ABOUT IT! As a class, agree on a topic for which you will interview others. Either from the following list or on your own, choose a topic on which people will have specific, interesting responses. Each person in the class should interview at least one or two other people. As a class, compose a list of ten questions. Individuals may add to the list during their interviews. Take notes on the interviews. Using the notes, discuss as a group the responses.

- What do you remember about the Civil Rights movement?
- What do you remember about John F. Kennedy's assassination?
- What do you remember about the day Pearl Harbor was bombed?
- What were your feelings and attitudes during the era of protest over Viet Nam?
- What do you remember about the Challenger explosion?
- How have schools changed since you were a student?

NOTETAKING

Taking notes from any resource means being fast and accurate. Taking notes correctly also avoids *plagiarism*, the use of someone else's words or ideas without giving credit. Plagiarism can take place in a speech as well as a book. You take notes rapidly, accurately, and honestly by following these steps:

1. *Skim.* Once you have located the source you think you want, skim it to see if it really has information related to your speech. If it does, immediately jot down the author, title, and date. All notes should be with this information so you can tell an audience where you found the material. Frequently, general information in reference books may be used without stating where it comes from.

2. *Paraphrase.* Unless the information must be quoted exactly, paraphrase it. That is, put it in your own words. In fact, writing the information in fragments is a good idea. You can put it into your own sentences later. Paraphrasing helps you avoid reading someone else's words to your audience. If you try to make others believe the words are your own when you are actually quoting someone, you are being dishonest and may lose the audience's belief in you as a speaker. Pay special attention to key phrases like "in other words," and "on the other hand." They tell you something important is coming up.

3. *Use "shorthand."* By using symbols and abbreviations you can speed up the note-taking process. Some symbols you might use are "+" for "and," and "=" for "the same as," "w/" for "with," "w/o" for "without," and so forth. Words used frequently can easily be shortened. If your speech is on radioactive waste, why not abbreviate the term "RAW" to save time in your notes?

4. *Keep your notes organized.* By keeping all notes on cards or in a folder, you will avoid losing important information.

ACTIVITY 3   Take notes on the following brief paragraph, using symbols and abbreviations. Then, without referring to the paragraph, use your notes to write another paragraph about the same subject.

A human being's reaction to death is one of psychology's most mysterious and interesting subjects. Perhaps we fear death too much to understand it well. The famous writer La Rochefoucald had a saying: "Man cannot look directly at the sun or death." Our inability to cope with death can be seen in various ways. We fear death enough to bury a body, but we care enough for the deceased to prepare the body elaborately for burial. The use of tombstones came from a fear that spirits would rise from the grave and stones would keep them weighed down. But we inscribed tombstones with words of honor and love. So complex is our response to death that it is studied by philosophers, ministers, doctors, authors, anthropologists, archeologists, and sociologists, as well as by psychologists and psychiatrists.

SPEAK UP!   Since this lesson is on research, you will use library materials to complete this assignment. First, choose a topic (or receive a topic assigned to you). Be sure it is a topic that is easily researched in the library. Then spend one class period in the library finding information on your subject. Take notes on the information.

During the next class period, you will be asked to give an outline speech on your topic. The speech should have a good organization, thesis, and topic development. Try to keep your speech between 2½ to 3½ minutes.

USING SOURCES RESPONSIBLY

After you've researched a speech and chosen materials to use, you must decide how to attribute them. Attributing means identifying the source of a quotation, statistic, opinion, or other piece of information. You will want to attribute your material for three reasons:

First, you attribute material to build your own credibility. If you are giving a speech on teenage employment, for example, you might want to show your audience that your information is supported by more than your experience and your opinion. By quoting a respected source (like the U.S. Department of Commerce, for example), you increase the likelihood that your audience will accept your information.

Second, you attribute material to build interest. If you can show that a famous, respected, or popular figure supports you, your audience may pay closer attention to your speech.

Third, you attribute material to give credit where credit is due. If you use someone's words directly or if you borrow an original idea, it is ethical to give the source of the words or idea. Attributing sources helps you avoid plagiarism.

This student followed all three guidelines in a speech on freedom of the press: When we celebrated the bicentennial of our Constitution, we celebrated 200 years of freedom of the press. We cannot risk taking the cherished freedom for granted. As New York Governor Mario Cuomo stated, we must "sound the alert...make it clear that we are facing a real threat of restriction of the constitutional freedom of the press. That's not easy."

If you are asked for a list of sources used in preparing a speech, you should prepare a bibliography. The exact style or form of a bibliography varies, but it always includes these things:

The author of a book, article, speech, or other source
The title of the source
The date of the source
Publication information, such as publisher, place of publication, editor, etc.

SUMMARY

If speakers only had to speak about themselves and their experiences and if they could instantly recall all important information, perhaps research would not be necessary. As speakers, we do have to speak on unfamiliar subjects, and because our audiences demand specific, lively information, we must use research. The library is usually the center of our research activities. By using the card catalog, the *Readers' Guide*, and the reference librarian, we can open up a wealth of new and interesting information. In addition, we can go outside the library and interview other people to gain information and other points of view. By noting our information carefully and using it correctly, we can improve the topic development of many of our speeches and reports. By attributing the materials we use, we can improve our presentations and we give credit where credit is due.

11

Organizing a Speech

```
I.  Major point
  A.  Subpoint
    1.  Example (subdivision
      a.  Additional example (
      (1)  Additional explana
        (a)  Additional expla
```

Picture This

Each year your school sponsors a student exchange with another school in the area. This year you will give a brief presentation explaining the layout of the school to the exchange students. Since they will be in the school for only a day, you know it is unnecessary to explain where every classroom or office is. You do not want to confuse them, nor do you want to leave out important information. You have several ways to organize the presentation. Which of the following choices will you select? Why?

A. Give each student a map of the building and point out important rooms floor by floor or wing by wing.
B. Explain the layout of the school according to its age. Begin with the original sections and then move to later additions.
C. Explain locations of rooms according to their purpose: math classrooms, English classrooms, etc., offices, media center, restrooms, commons area, cafeteria, gym.
D. Find out where they will go throughout the day and then explain the building according to where students will be at different times during the day.

INTRODUCTION:　Organizing a Speech

Each of the options listed in "Picture This . . ." has merits. Regardless of which option you choose, your speech will have order. The most important thing to remember when organizing a speech is that there must be a framework for ordering ideas. In "Picture This . . .," option *A* was organized by dividing the school into spaces or areas and discussing each in a logical order such as from first floor to third floor or from wing A to wing D. Options *B* and *D* used a different organizing principle—time. Option *B* organized the information according to the age of various parts of the building. Option *D* organized according to the students' schedules during the day. Option *C* classified rooms according to their purposes.

Each of these frameworks, as well as others, will be discussed in this lesson. Additionally, you will learn how to use an outline to prepare your speaking notes and how to develop transitions to move smoothly from one idea to another.

THE PARTS OF A SPEECH

By this point you have probably determined that all speeches have three major parts: introduction, body, and conclusion. Each part of a speech serves a different function. In the next lesson we will discuss the purposes of introductions and conclusions. In this lesson we will concentrate on the heart of the speech, the body. Speakers often organize the material in the body of the speech before they prepare an introduction and conclusion. This is a good way for beginning speakers to approach speech writing.

In preparing the body of the speech, you must consider your purpose, both general and specific. As you will learn later, your general purpose of informing, persuading, or entertaining will influence how you order your ideas.

The body of the speech is the longest part of the speech. This is where you present your information. The introduction prepares an audience for what is to be presented in the body and the conclusion summarizes the major ideas. Since the body of the speech is the major part, you must give it the greatest amount of preparation. Once you decide on a topic, narrow it, and research it, you must organize the material. There are three steps involved in this process: (1) selecting an organizational pattern, (2) outlining the content, and (3) preparing the transitions.

ORGANIZATIONAL PATTERNS

There is no single way to organize a speech. The pattern you select will be determined by the information you have and the specific purpose you want to achieve. There are six basic patterns for organizing a speech:

1. Logical or topical
2. Chronological
3. Spatial
4. Classification
5. Problem-solution
6. Cause-effect

Logical or Topical Order

Logical or topical organization is one of the most common patterns. It is especially useful for informative and entertainment speeches. This pattern is used when you have several ideas to present and one idea seems naturally to precede the other. A speech about the benefits of exercise would fit this category. You might include the following ideas in this order:

I. Physical benefits
   A. Cardiovascular strength
   B. Muscle tone
   C. Weight loss
II. Mental benefits
   A. You are more alert
   B. You feel better about yourself

Since we consider exercise to be for the body, it seems more logical to begin with the physical benefits of exercise. There is no reason, however, why you could not reverse I and II, but they seem to fit more logically in the order presented.

Chronological Order

Another word for *chronological* is *time*. The pattern of chronological order organizes by using time sequence as a framework. Two of the examples in "Picture This . . ." used a time sequence as the organizing principle. This type of pattern is useful in informative speeches or in persuasive speeches which require background information on a problem or issue. A speech on the history of baseball could use a chronological sequence. You would begin with the invention of the game and follow rule changes until the present day.

Chronological order is also useful for a process or demonstration speech. Each of these speeches involves explanation of how to do something. In a process speech, you explain but actually do not show how to do what you are explaining. In a demonstration, you explain by showing. For the demonstration to make sense, you must follow the order in which things are done.

Spatial Order

Spatial order involves physical space. If you were to describe your classroom, you might describe what is found in the front of the room, the back, the sides, and the center. Dividing material according to spaces in the room would use spatial order. Many television reporters use spatial order. The national weather report is usually given according to regions of the country. A weather reporter does not randomly skip from one city to another.

Spatial order is often used in informative speeches and, depending upon the topic, it is appropriate for entertainment speeches. Use this organizational pattern whenever physical space is involved. Section material by floors, parts of a room, geographical region, etc.

Classification

Classification order requires you to put things into categories or classes. Students are distinguished by their year in school. This is a type of classification. The example of describing the rooms in the school according to their purpose was a type of classification. This pattern is useful for all three speech purposes. Solutions to problems can be categorized according to type. Information is easily given by classifying ideas. This lesson, for example, uses a classification system to explain organizational patterns.

ACTIVITY 1   For each of the following speech topics, write the organizational pattern that would be most appropriate. Explain your choice.

1. Aviation—from the Wright brothers to the moon

2. Training a dog to sit and roll over

3. Types of defenses in basketball

4. The nations that are members of the United Nations

5. Development of the movie industry

6. Propaganda techniques used in television commercials

A. Logical or topical

B. Chronological

C. Spatial

D. Classification

Problem-Solution Order   Most often speakers use problem-solution order for persuasive speeches. The first part of such a speech outlines a problem, and the second part gives a solution. Within a problem-solution pattern you will find other types of organization. The problem section of the speech might be organized using a logical sequence. The solution stage could involve classification. As a persuader, you would select one solution and present arguments for why it is the best option. A speech about the decline of educational quality in the United States would include a section outlining the problems in U.S. schools, and the next section would suggest ways to solve them.

Cause-Effect Order   The cause-effect pattern, like the problem-solution pattern, has two parts. The first describes the cause of a problem and the second its effects. You could organize a speech on toxic waste pollution by using a cause-effect pattern. The first part of the speech might explain how and why toxic wastes cause environmental damage. The second part would discuss the effects of toxic wastes on property and health. As with the problem-solution speech, other forms of organization are usually incorporated into the major sections.

SPEAK UP!   Select one of the following topics and use the organizational pattern in parentheses to prepare a two- to three-minute speech. The speech should have a brief introduction, which includes your purpose statement, and a conclusion, which summarizes your main points.

1. Describe the biggest problem you faced this week and tell how you solved it. (Problem-solution)

2. Explain why your grades in a class went up or down. (Cause-effect)

3. Explain what you do during a typical day. (Chronological)

4. Describe a room in your home. (Spatial)

5. Explain how you spend your entertainment dollars. (Either logical or classification)

6. Describe people in your school or your place of work according to their year in school or their job category. (Classification).

Multiple Patterns As with the problem-solution and cause-effect patterns, a speech may use more than one organizing pattern. Most speeches, in fact, do use a combination. While the total speech may use a logical pattern, each individual section might incorporate a separate scheme. The following outline illustrates how multiple patterns are used:

General Purpose: To inform
Specific Purpose: The purpose of this speech is to increase my classmates' understanding of the compact disc.

Body

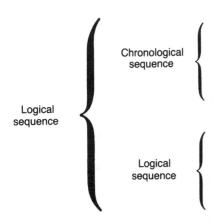

Logical sequence

Chronological sequence

I. Development of compact disc technology
   A. Digitalization of information
   B. Invention of the laser
   C. First CD player
   D. Portable "compact" CD player

Logical sequence

II. Advantages of compact discs
   A. More information in less space
   B. Almost indestructible
   C. Clarity of sound
   D. Random access

This is not a complete outline since specific details are missing, but it gives you an idea of how to mix organizational formats within a single speech.

Organization Relates to Purpose By changing the organization of material, you can change the general purpose. If you were to take the topic of exercise, you could use a classification system and present an informative speech describing three or four major types of exercise. A chronological sequence, explaining how to perform one particular type of exercise, would turn the topic into a process or demonstration speech. A problem-solution pattern that began by talking about people with health problems due to lack of exercise and that concluded by telling how to make exercise a part of your daily schedule would be a persuasive speech. A logical pattern describing humorous incidents a person experienced while exercising would help organize an entertainment speech.

ACTIVITY 2 For one speech assignment, you gave a demonstration speech. Using the topic for that speech, select an organizing pattern and prepare rough outlines for an informative and either a persuasive or an entertainment speech.

Include the speech purpose for each type of speech and briefly explain how you chose the organizing pattern for each one.

PRINCIPLES OF OUTLINING

By now you have seen many examples of outlines or partial outlines. While these examples give you a general idea of how to write an outline, they are not complete outlines. In this section you will learn the steps in outlining so you can write and use an outline as a speaking guide.

Rules of Outlining

An outline is an abbreviated way of presenting information for a speech. It helps you organize ideas and it provides key words and phrases to jog your memory as you speak. Outlines have a standard format—they are not randomly structured. The following are guidelines for constructing an outline.

1. Use standard subordination

The most general information should be the first step in an outline. The major points of a speech should be labeled with Roman numerals (*I, II, III*, etc.). Each item under a major point should relate directly to and explain the major point. These items are known as subpoints. Examples, statistics, and explanations become subdivisions of the subpoints. The process of dividing material into more specific information is known as *subordination*. The standard format for subordination is as follows:

  I. Major point
     A. Subpoint
        1. Example (subdivision of subpoint)
           a. Additional example or explanation
              (1) Additional explanation
                 (a) Additional explanation

Each level of subordination should be indented as shown in this example. As a general rule, if you have a Roman number *I*, you should have a *II*. If you have an *A* point, you should also have a *B*. Since each level of subordination indicates you are dividing a topic to make it more specific, it is assumed you have more than one idea to divide. If you do not, then you need to reexamine the way you have organized your material.

Your outlines will rarely go beyond the third level of subordination. For an average ten-minute speech, you should be able to cover from two to five major points. Three major points are about right for a five-minute speech.

2. Use one statement per unit of subordination

The purpose of an outline is to break information into its simplest form. Each level or unit of an outline is in its simplest form and should include only one idea, example, or illustration.

Wrong: A. Early CD players and new portables
Right: A. Early CD players
        B. Portable CD players

If the outline were structured as in the incorrect example, you would not know if a subpoint or example under *A* referred to early CD players or to the newer portable models.

3. Do not overlap items

There is more than one way to divide or classify material. Be sure your information is subdivided so each unit is distinct from other levels. For instance,

Wrong: A. Parents are affected
        B. People with no children are affected
        C. Married people are affected
Right: A. Parents are affected
          1. Married parents
          2. Single parents
        B. People with no children are affected
          1. Married individuals
          2. Single individuals

In the first example, subpoint *C* could include both parents (*A*) and people with no children (*B*). In the correct example, you can easily distinguish between people who have children (*A—1,2*) and people who do not have children (*B—1,2*).

4. Give equal value to ideas on the same level of subordination

Each level should relate consistently to a category of information. All Roman numerals should represent major points; all uppercase letters should represent general subdivisions; and all Arabic numerals should represent examples. You should not mix types of examples as in the following:

Wrong:

A.　Major industries are affected by imported cars
　　1.　Shipping
　　2.　Steel
　　3.　Ford Motor Company

Ford Motor Company is out of place because it is not a major industry. It is a corporation *within a major industry*: automobile manufacturing. The correct subordination would be:

Right:

A.　Major industries are affected by imported cars
　　1.　Shipping
　　2.　Steel
　　3.　Automobile
　　　　a.　Ford Motor Company
　　　　b.　Chrysler
　　　　c.　General Motors

5. Use complete sentences for major points

Many beginning speakers write too much and read large portions of an outline if they write complete sentences for every level. They can speak more effectively if they use complete sentences only for major ideas and transitions within the outline. Examples, statistics, or illustrations can be indicated with words or phrases and are easier to see during a speech.

6. Outline each section of the speech separately

The introduction and conclusion should be outlined with major points beginning with Roman numeral *I*. The first major point in the body should also be given a Roman numeral *I* designation. In most speeches, however, you will write out the introduction and conclusion and will outline only the body.

TRANSITIONAL DEVICES

Transitions are the threads that tie the parts of your speech together. On page 42 is a partial outline that includes transitional material. As you will notice, transitional material helps you move smoothly from one idea to another. Transitions show the relationship of one idea to the idea that follows.

There are two general types of transitions—internal and external. *Internal transitions* relate information within a section of a speech, such as relating three motor companies under the general heading of "automobile industry."

The following words are common internal transitions:

Also	For example
And	Specifically
But	Again
Or	One other
Another	In other words
In addition	Since
However	Then

External transitions connect points on different levels of an outline. For instance, they would show the relationship between the major points labelled with Roman numerals. External transitions usually include more than a word or phrase. They show relationships as well as a change in direction. They also highlight the most important points. Some common external transitions are:

The final reason for change is...
The most important point I want to make is...
Now, what effect does this have on...
The second step in the process is...
Those are the problems; now what can be done about them?

After you have experience as a speaker, your transitions will come naturally. As a beginning speaker, however, it is advisable to prepare your external transitions.

TALK ABOUT IT!   In small groups, select a speech either from this book or from another source. Read the speech together and then make one list of the internal transitions and a second list of the external transitions. Compare your lists with those of other groups.

A COMPLETED OUTLINE

General Purpose: To inform

Specific Purpose: The purpose of this speech is to increase science fiction readers' and nonreaders' understanding of the relationship between science fiction and science.

Thesis: When speaking of science fiction as a prediction of the future direction of science, two authors surface as the leaders in this art—Isaac Asimov and George Orwell.

Introduction: Why do we read science fiction? Is it because it allows us to escape from reality? Or do we read it because it is actually one of the many steps in the scientific process? Does science fiction predict what the future of science will be? I think many of us read science fiction because it does provide us with insights into the future. Our parents and grandparents remember Buck

Rogers as fiction and fantasy, but we have grown up with manned flight through space and footsteps on the moon.

When speaking of science fiction as a prediction of the future, two authors surface as the leaders in this art—Isaac Asimov and George Orwell. I would like to share with you some of their predictions and then let you determine why we read science fiction.

Body

Transition to Body: One of the most popular ideas to come out of science fiction is the robot, and Isaac Asimov is the man who told us the most about them in "I, Robot."

   I. Isaac Asimov predicted the use of robots
      A. Asimov predicted robots would be used in industry
      B. Asimov predicted robots would be used in medicine
      C. Asimov predicted robots would look like machines, not like metal people

Transition: If we look around us, we will see that Asimov wasn't far off in his predictions.

   II. Asimov's predictions have come true
      A. Industry uses robots
         1. Automobile industry
         2. Space industry
      B. Medical technology uses computerized limbs for amputees

Transition: These are but a few uses of robotics. Scientists tell us robots will replace more and more people on assembly lines. However, not all science fiction predictions involve such intricate technology as robots. George Orwell predicted many scientific and technical changes in our everyday lives.

   III. Orwell had many valid predictions
      A. He predicted use of data banks
      B. He predicted word processors
      C. He predicted satellites

   IV. Orwell's predictions have come true
      A. Data banks know much about us
      B. Word processors are common
      C. Satellites circle the earth daily
         1. Weather
         2. Telecommunications
         3. Military

Transition: These are but a few of the science fictions that have become facts. Many others have not.

Conclusion: One scientist has estimated that only ten percent of all science fiction can be taken as prophecy. However, that ten percent, as Asimov and Orwell have shown us, can have a major impact on our lives.

SUMMARY

The body of the speech is the heart of your presentation. The material in the body must be well organized and clear. Regardless of the general purpose of your speech, you can choose one of several patterns of organization: logical, chronological, spatial, classification, problem-solution, and cause-effect.

Most speeches use a combination of organizational patterns. It is important to outline your ideas to guarantee that you are using the most effective patterns. You should follow standard outlining procedures in preparing a speech. An outline should serve as a reminder of your major ideas.

A completed outline should also include transitions to tie your material together and make your speech flow from one idea to the next. Through a combination of internal and external transitions, your speech will have unity and smoothness.

12

Introductions & Conclusions

Picture This . . .

You are in an audience waiting to hear a speech. Which of the following introductions would get your attention and make you want to listen to the speech?

Introduction A

It's later this afternoon. You and a friend have stopped at a nearby restaurant for a snack. As you laugh about the prank you played on a friend earlier in the day, you hear someone yell, "Help! Oh, no. I think she's dying!"

You look up to see people scrambling out of their chairs. They are all headed in the direction of a woman who is choking. Everyone is running around. No one is doing anything. But you listened to this speech so you know what to do. You know about the Heimlich Maneuver and you become the hero of the day.

Introduction B

Everyone eats. And every time we put food in our mouths we run the risk of choking. Many people die each year from choking on food. Today I want to teach you how to save the life of a person who is choking.

Why did you choose one introduction over the other? Which of the following factors makes an introduction effective?

A. It is short and to the point.
B. It says clearly what the speaker will discuss.
C. It gets your attention and arouses your interest.
D. It relates the topic to the audience.
E. It includes a joke.

INTRODUCTION: Introductions and Conclusions

If you selected introduction *A* as your choice in "Picture This . . .," it was probably because it kept you in suspense. It grabbed your interest and held it. You did not know for the first few lines where the speaker was taking you. The introduction made you want to hear more.

A speaker must capture an audience's interest immediately. If listeners' minds begin to stray at the beginning of the speech, it will be difficult to regain their attention.

It is also important to leave an audience on a good note. The conclusion should be as memorable as the introduction. In fact, the introduction and conclusion tie the entire speech together and give it unity. They make the speech whole rather than three separate parts: introduction, body, conclusion.

In this lesson you will learn about the purposes of introductions and conclusions, as well as techniques for preparing them.

PURPOSES OF INTRODUCTIONS

The primary purpose of an introduction is to state the topic of your speech. However, the introduction should be more than a statement such as "Today I am going to give you advice on how to find a summer job." While that statement clearly establishes your purpose, it does not make your audience sit up and want to listen.

A good introduction gets the audience's attention. One way to do this is to make the audience aware of how important the topic is to them. For example, young people are not worried about stress and high blood pressure, but the dietary and behavioral habits that cause stress-related diseases start early in life. A good introduction would make audience members realize this and want to learn more about stress. The following is an introduction to a speech on stress. Notice how it gets attention, makes the topic important to the listeners, and states the topic.

How many of you get impatient while waiting in a slow-moving line at a movie? Do you ever get behind with school work because you have too many outside activities? How often do you eat a meal on the run? If you answered "yes" to the first two questions and "more than once or twice a week" to the third, you may be on your way to developing a stress-related disease by the time you are in your forties. Forty may seem like a long way off, and the situations I described may seem normal for students, but some individuals are prone to creating situations which cause more stress in their lives than is normal. Today, I want to discuss stress—what it is, what it can do to you, and what you can do to reduce it before it gets the better of you.

As you have learned, every speech must have a thesis statement. In the introduction on stress, the last sentence is a thesis statement. It serves as a forecast of the major points in the speech. This sentence lets listeners know exactly what will be covered. If this speech were outlined, the points noted with Roman numerals would correspond to the points in the forecast:

   I. What is stress?
  II. What does stress do to your body?
 III. What can you do to reduce stress in your life?

> A good introduction should do five things:
> 1. Introduce the topic
> 2. Get the audience's attention
> 3. Make the audience aware of the topic's importance
> 4. Present the thesis
> 5. Forecast the major points in the speech

ACTIVITY 1   Examine the introductions to at least three speeches you have given or read. Identify and write the lines containing the following in each introduction:

1. The attention getter

2. The topic

3. The topic's importance

4. The thesis

5. The forecast

Are any of these missing in any of the introductions? Would the introduction be better with the missing information? Rewrite one of the introductions to include all five elements.

In addition to the five elements of a good introduction, there are four other purposes an introduction can have under certain circumstances. They are:

1. Establish the speaker's credibility
2. Promote good will
3. Establish common ground
4. Set a tone

Establish Credibility   Unless speakers are well-known experts, an audience may need proof of their qualifications to speak on a subject. In situations where the audience knows nothing about your expertise, it is important to establish your credibility or believability. Through personal reference, a speaker can let an audience know he or she has personal experience or has researched the subject. Often when a speaker is introduced to a group, the person who introduces the speaker provides the background to establish credibility. In a classroom setting, this will not happen. Credibility can be established with as little as one sentence in the introduction. In a speech on job-hunting skills, the speaker might want to insert the following sentence to establish credibility:

By following the guidelines I am going to share with you, I was able to find a summer job after spending only two days of looking and interviewing.

In addition to using the introduction to establish credibility, a speaker should also include sources of information and additional personal references throughout the speech to enhance this credibility.

Promote Good Will   Occasionally speakers address hostile audiences or audiences that disagree. When this happens, the speaker needs to assure the audience there will be no cause for further disagreement. When the President of the United States takes office and presents an inaugural address, an attempt is made to bring the country together after an election. Even though some voters did not vote for the winner, the President needs everyone's support during the next four years. One goal of this speech could be described as promoting good will.

Establish Common Ground

There are times when we think we have little in common with a famous speaker or even with people we know. It is important to remind an audience that we all have something in common. You may not think a teacher who tells you how to overcome fear of public speaking knows how you feel. After all, a teacher talks to groups every day. However, that teacher probably does know what you are going through because he or she was a beginner at one time. By relating personal experiences, a speaker establishes a common bond with the listeners and gives the speech new meaning.

Set a Tone

The tone or mood of a speech is important. If you are giving a humorous speech, you want everyone to relax and enjoy it. Your introduction can establish the tone you want. By using humor, you let the audience know the speech will be light. By using a serious quotation from a philosopher, you let the audience know you have an important topic to discuss. If you are to accomplish your purpose, you must prepare the audience for your message, and the introduction can assist you in doing that.

TALK ABOUT IT!

Working in groups, list one or more introduction purposes (A. establish credibility, B. promote good will, C. establish common ground, or D. set a tone) for each of the following situations:

1. A former gang member speaking to a group of students about violence in schools.

2. A sixteen-year-old student giving a persuasive speech on the importance of voting in U.S. elections.

3. A high school graduate giving a speech on the value of studying.

4. A volunteer worker appealing to a group of wealthy people to give money to support the homeless in the community.

5. The town mayor giving the opening address at the Fourth of July festivities.

TYPES OF INTRODUCTIONS

A good speech does *not* begin with the following:

"Today I want to talk about bicycle maintenance."

"My speech is about calligraphy—the art of handwriting."

"My topic is how to buy a pet."

While the topic is clear in all of these statements, the opening sentence does not create excitement about the topic. You can use several techniques to fulfill your introduction purposes and add some life to your introductions. Six of the most common techniques are:

1. Quotation
2. Rhetorical question or series of questions
3. Reference to history, audience, or self
4. Humor
5. Startling statement
6. Incident

Quotation

Using a quotation is a common way to open a speech. You can find material in speeches, novels, poetry, or books of quotations. Often someone else has said something that makes a point better than you can. A quotation can also add credibility to your speech—not only do you think something, but someone famous does as well. The following is an opening using a quotation:

President John F. Kennedy once said, "The United States must move very fast to even stand still." Since President Kennedy made that observation over thirty years ago, the advances in technology have made it even more important for this country to prepare its students for a competitive world.

Rhetorical Question

A rhetorical question is a question to which a speaker does not expect an answer. It is asked to stimulate the audience's thinking. A speaker can use a single question or a series. The introduction to the speech on stress used a series of rhetorical questions.

Personal and Historical References

References are used to establish common ground or to aid credibility. Historical references are used when a speech is being given on a special occasion. Martin Luther King, Jr. used historical reference in the introduction to his ''I Have a Dream'' speech:

Five score years ago, a great American, in whose symbolic shadow we stand today, signed the Emancipation Proclamation.

The following is an example of an introduction using an audience reference:

Everyone in this audience knows what it is like to take a test. Everyone knows what it is like to be called on by a teacher in class. As students, we expect to be questioned and quizzed about our studies. But have you ever thought that once we leave school and get jobs we are also going to be tested and quizzed?

An introduction using a personal reference, or reference to self, might look something like this:

Forty years ago when I was graduated from high school, the world was a different place than it is for graduates today. Computers had not taken over the world. Students did not have to prepare to change jobs or careers at least six times in their lives.

Humor

Humor can be used in most speeches, even those with a serious message. It might seem contradictory, but it is possible to set a serious tone by using humor. When speakers contrast the seriousness of a problem with the lightness of a joke, they can emphasize a message quickly.

Humor should always be in good taste. It should not offend individuals or groups. Before you tell a joke or humorous story, ask yourself if anyone might be offended. If there is any doubt in your mind, either change the story or joke or do not use it.

A speech on the need for commitment to goals may begin with humor:

Many of us have enjoyed steak and eggs for breakfast. But have we ever thought about the roles of the chicken and the steer in our breakfast? They aren't the same. The chicken was *involved*, but the steer was definitely *committed* to feeding us! Often our commitment is more like the chicken's—we are involved in the process, but not really committed all the way.

Startling Statement   A startling statement grabs our attention by making us think of something in a way we had not considered or by shocking us. Often a topic that might sound boring to an audience can be made more interesting through the use of a startling statement. Consider the following example:

Stop! Before you take another bite out of a peanut butter and jelly sandwich, think about the fact that it may be slowly killing you. How? Simple. There is a natural substance in peanuts known as aflatoxin that could cause cancer. But then, you ask, what in our food doesn't cause cancer?

After this opening, you definitely want to hear the rest of the speech before you open your sack lunch. A startling statement is a good way to fulfill the purposes of getting an audience's attention and making them aware of the importance of a subject.

Incident   The final technique of starting an introduction is the use of incident. By telling about an incident, you relate a situation to the audience and provide a concrete example of an occurrence or situation directly related to your topic. This type of introduction can provide a vivid picture for the audience and can involve them quickly. The following is an example of incident:

Last week a young boy was hovering near death in a hospital room across town. As his parents prepared to accept the fact their son would be with them only a few more hours, they made a decision which would help him live on. They decided to donate their son's organs so that others might live or at least live fuller lives. Today, two individuals are recipients of kidneys which will free them from dialysis machines, a woman is on her way to seeing again, and a young child will receive a liver which will save her from a rare disease.

SPEAK UP!   Using a speech you have given or read, rewrite the introduction two ways. Label the introduction technique you used for each one. Underline the thesis and forecast.

Present one of the two introductions orally to a classmate for critique.

CONCLUSIONS

Just as a speech should begin on a high note, it should also have a definite, positive ending. It should not just come to a stop. A good speech does not require a speaker to say "That's all" or "I'm finished." The audience knows the speech is over and knows what the speaker expects of them as a result.

A good conclusion should do three things:

1. Inform the audience you are about to close
2. Summarize the major ideas
3. Leave the audience with an idea to remember

The first objective is achieved by using transitional devices. The speaker needs to connect the final point of the body to the conclusion. Examine the completed outline on pages 94–95. Note how the speaker connected the last line of the body to the conclusion.

These are but a few of the science fictions that have become facts. Many others have not.

One scientist has estimated that only ten percent of all science fiction can be taken as prophecy. . . If that is true, then why do we read science fiction?

Once the speaker asked, "Why do we read science fiction?" he indicated he was about to summarize the reasons given in the speech. The speaker had asked a similar question in the introduction and had given the reasons in the body. Now the speaker let the audience know that he would reemphasize and summarize the main points in the conclusion. The speech had come full circle and listeners knew it was about to end.

There is an old adage that the introduction tells listeners what the speaker is going to tell them, the body tells them, and the conclusion tells the audience what the speaker has told them. By emphasizing major ideas three times, a speaker gives an audience a clear understanding of the speech's intent. Repetition is an effective way of teaching, and in speechmaking it is an effective way of getting a point across. Thus, a summary of major ideas is essential in a conclusion.

Look at the conclusion to the demonstration speech on page 62. Find the summary. Does the summary emphasize the points outlined in the introduction?

In addition to summarizing content, a speaker also wants to make a point with the audience. The speaker may want to conclude by issuing a challenge to the audience or by leaving them with a vivid picture. If you use a memorable statement, you help your audience remember the thesis of the speech long after it is over.

ACTIVITY 2   Look at the conclusion to the same speech you used in SPEAK UP! Identify the lines that contain a transition to the conclusion, the summary, and a point for the audience to remember. Are any of these missing from the conclusion? Rewrite it to meet the three objectives of a good conclusion.

TYPES OF CONCLUSIONS

There are several techniques for concluding a speech that will enable a speaker to fulfill the three major purposes of a conclusion.

Generally, anything that can be used to begin a speech can also be used to conclude it. A quotation can serve as a memorable statement. A rhetorical question can serve as a transition from the body to the conclusion. An incident can leave the audience with a vivid picture to illustrate your thesis one last time. A personal reference can serve as a challenge.

Most speakers try to tie the introduction back into the conclusion. If a conclusion were prepared for the speech on personal commitment, the speaker could relate back to the steak and eggs example:

So next time you volunteer for a project or set a personal goal, think about the chicken and the steer. Are you going to be involved but give little of yourself, or are you going to be committed and give it everything you have? Success or failure can be the difference.

SUMMARY

As with anything else in life, getting started properly can make a difference in the final product. A good introduction serves five purposes: it introduces the topic, gets attention, states the thesis, forecasts the major points in the body, and makes the audience understand the topic's importance to them.

There are several techniques a speaker can use to begin a speech. Each technique helps meet one or more of the purposes for an introduction. The six most common strategies are: quotation, rhetorical question, references, humor, startling statement, and incident.

A conclusion can use any of the strategies used in an introduction. Regardless of the techniques used, the conclusion should do three things: inform the audience the speech is drawing to a close, summarize the main points, and leave the audience with something to remember.

13

The Informative Speech

Picture This . . .

You are required to give a speech, eight to ten minutes long, presenting recent information on a newsworthy topic. You may use notes. The audience will be people your age. Your evaluation will be based on your research, preparation, and delivery.

Since the topics you know most about—sports and music—are not allowed, you have chosen a topic that you are not familiar with: alternative energy sources. Fortunately, the library has a great deal of recent information about energy sources. You have done some research, and you have made good notes. Now you must decide how to present the information. What will you do?

A. Present a lot of recent statistics on cost and amount of energy produced through traditional and alternative sources.
B. Collect clippings on energy from recent newspapers. Read and explain each one to the class.
C. Report on one long article about a nuclear power plant that will be finished in five years.
D. Use a science textbook and report on how various types of energy are produced.
E. Review the current debate on fossil fuels and present it to the class in a pro and con fashion.

INTRODUCTION: The Informative Speech

While we are students we are probably most familiar with the informative speech. We listen to them in the form of lectures and we give them in the form of class presentations, projects, and book reports. If you have given a report of any kind recently, you know firsthand that an informative speech requires you to present new information in an interesting manner.

Often the problem is not one of finding information; the real problem is selecting what you want to use and finding a good way to present it.

In applying what you learn about the informative speech, you will also use what you know about the basics of public speaking. Now you will learn the different methods of presenting information, beginning with a sample speech.

A SAMPLE INFORMATIVE SPEECH

For this sample speech, assume the following: The speech was written to meet the requirements of a history class. The teacher required a five- to six-minute speech on a major incident in twentieth-century American history. The speech was to be prepared with library materials and finished within one week. The audience members were the other students in the class, but only the teacher would evaluate the speech.

After choosing an interesting topic (the invention of the atomic bomb) and doing some research, the student identified a specific purpose and thesis.

Purpose: The purpose of this speech is to inform the class about the exciting race from 1939 to 1945 to build the first atomic bomb.

Thesis: Although it was part science and part history, the story of the Manhattan Project is also an adventure as exciting as anything Hollywood could produce.

Organization   Since the speech is about a historical event and the period leading to it, the student chose a chronological organization—that is, an organization that follows an arrangement according to time.

Knowing the audience helped the student choose an introduction and conclusion. The introduction would refer to adventure and science fiction movies. The conclusion would refer to the growing concern over nuclear war. Both these topics were well known to the audience.

This is an outline of the speech:

The Adventure of the Manhattan Project

Thesis: Although it was part science and part history, the story of the Manhattan Project is also an adventure as exciting as anything Hollywood could produce.

I. Introduction
   A. Comparing the Manhattan Project to a movie script
   B. Thesis

II. The Beginning of the Adventure—1939
   A. The German research
   B. Enrico Fermi's realization
   C. Einstein's plea to President Roosevelt

III. The Development of an Atomic Pile
    A. The need for a controlled chain reaction
    B. Comparing the reaction to stacking dominoes
    C. The materials used in the secret project

IV. Producing Nuclear Materials for the Bomb
    A. Three methods used
    B. Statistics on the cost

V. Los Alamos—1944–1945
    A. The purpose of the Los Alamos laboratory
    B. The first experimental blast
        1. The results
        2. 20,000 tons of TNT
        3. Oppenheimer's reaction

VI. The End of the War
    A. Truman's decision
    B. The results of the Hiroshima bomb and the Nagasaki bomb
    C. The surrender

VII. Conclusion—The Race Was Over
    A. Total cost
    B. A new kind of war
    C. First heroes of the atomic age

Research   The materials used to build this speech could be found in almost any library:

The Encyclopaedia Britannica
The Physicists by Daniel J. Kevles
The Glory and the Dream by William Manchester
Rise of the American Nation, new 2nd Ed., by Lewis Paul Todd and Merle Curti

The Adventure of the Manhattan Project

Examples   For just a moment forget that you are a student of history. Imagine you are a Hollywood director responsible for a multi-million dollar movie like *Terminator II* or *Aliens III*. The script you are given has this plot: A huge war is raging between an evil army and a good army. The war has engulfed the entire civilization. As the war continues to take millions of lives, the most brilliant scientists on each side are racing to build a top secret superweapon, a weapon so terrible and destructive that it will guarantee victory to whoever has it—if it doesn't destroy both sides. At the end of the script, the good army achieves a breakthrough, and in a display of power unlike anything in history, the superweapon ends the war in eight days.

Does it sound like science fiction? Too far out to make a good movie? Too unrealistic? The plot may be too far out for Hollywood, but it is the true story of the Manhattan Project, America's incredible development of the **Thesis** first atomic bomb during World War II. Although it was part science and part history, the story of the Manhattan Project is also an adventure as exciting as anything Hollywood could produce.

It is hard to say where the adventure starts. Scientists throughout the first part of the twentieth century had been exploring the atom. In the late **Fact** 1930s, however, a German and an Austrian published a scientific paper which set minds in America to thinking. The Germans, who had already

Incident begun their conquest of Europe, had shown that an atomic bomb was possible. One scientist who read the paper in 1939 was Enrico Fermi, who had left Italy to escape Hitler's ally, Mussolini. According to another scientist who shared Fermi's New York office, Fermi gazed out over New York City, spread his arms as if he held an imaginary ball, and remarked that a bomb that size could make the whole city disappear. The race to build the bomb—and possibly to win the war—was on.

Facts But how could the scientists convince the politicians to begin the long and costly research? Into the adventure stepped the twentieth century's greatest scientist. On August 2, 1939, Albert Einstein met with President Franklin Delano Roosevelt and warned him of the new weapon and Nazi Germany's research. F.D.R. approved spending $6,000 to begin an investigation into the possibility of building an atom bomb. Three years later the project started. It was code-named the Manhattan Project.

Analogy Before a bomb could be built, a controlled chain reaction had to take place. That means that enough atoms had to split to cause more atoms to split, and so on until the process kept itself going. Like a very complicated arrangement of dominoes, one atom caused several others to split and release their energy. Fermi and the scientists working at the University of Chicago started a secret project near an abandoned athletic field at the *Statistics* university. Using 400 tons of graphite (which is like the lead in a pencil), 12,000 pounds of uranium metal, and 100,000 pounds of uranium oxide, the scientists succeeded in creating a controlled chain reaction.

Facts The original $6,000 investment ballooned into a $400,000,000 investment. The money was needed to fund three different plans of producing the nuclear materials for the bomb. Scientists did not know which method would work, so all three had to be tried. Each project worked as fast as possible. *Analogy* One source called the three-project competition a "nightmarish horserace." *Statistics* One project alone required 28,000,000 pounds of silver worth $400,000,000. The silver was borrowed from the U.S. Treasury.

Opinion Many scientists worked in several different locations to turn out the materials for the bomb. The greatest challenge, however, lay with the scientists working in Los Alamos, New Mexico. J. Robert Oppenheimer was in charge of a staff of the most talented physicists and engineers in *Fact* America. It was their job to build and test the bomb itself. The project was so secret that birth certificates of babies born to the scientists' families had no real place of birth listed.

Working on problems no scientist had ever confronted before, the staff raced to complete the bomb. The war in Europe was over, but the war in the Pacific still claimed American lives.

Fact On July 16, 1945, before sunrise, the first experimental A-bomb was detonated. First, a flash of light brightened the darkness. Next, a shockwave and a huge roar tore at the onlookers more than 10,000 meters away. *Statistics* The scientists had predicted a blast equal to 5,000 tons of TNT. Instead, the blast was equal to 20,000 tons of TNT.

Scientists had no way of knowing exactly what was happening at the center of the explosion, but Oppenheimer observed the scene and recalled *Quotation* a line from a Hindu holy work: "I am become Death, the shatterer of worlds."

President Harry Truman (who had not even been briefed on the Manhattan Project until he became President when Roosevelt died) *Facts* decided that the atom bomb could force a Japanese surrender. On August 6, 1945, a United States B-29 named *Enola Gay* dropped the first atomic

Statistics   bomb, code-named Little Boy, on Hiroshima, Japan. Everything in the immediate vicinity of the blast was completely destroyed. An area of 4.4 square miles was completely burned out. Between 70,000 and 80,000 people died.

Fact   On August 9, a second bomb, code-named Fat Man, was dropped on Nagasaki with similar results.

Fact   On August 10, eight days after the first bomb, the Japanese surrendered. The war was over.

And the race was over. The Manhattan Project ushered in the Atomic Age.

After two billion dollars, six years, countless work hours, and more scientific genius than had ever been accumulated at one time in human history, the script was written.

And a new kind of war more horrible than ever before had been invented. In 1947, Secretary of War Henry Stimson summed up how the Manhattan Project had changed our lives:

Quotation/ Opinion   "The face of war is the face of death. . . . War in the twentieth century has grown steadily more barbarous, more destructive, more debased in all its aspects. Now, with the release of atomic energy, man's ability to destroy himself is very nearly complete. The bombs dropped on Hiroshima and Nagasaki ended a war. They also made it wholly clear that we must never have another war."

Despite the controversy over nuclear weapons, one thing is sure. The Manhattan Project is a story of men and women committed to scientific discovery and patriotism. It is a story worth retelling.

TYPES OF PROOF

The sample speech meets the requirements of the assignment. It also is an interesting speech. Let us look at how the speaker presented the information.

Facts   Almost all informative speeches depend on presenting facts. Facts can be proven true. Many facts are given in the speech; for example, the dates and the names are facts. How many examples of facts are in the speech?

Opinion   An opinion differs from a fact in that an opinion can be proven or disproven. The speaker's belief that the Manhattan Project is exciting is an example of an opinion. What other opinions are presented?

Statistics   Statistics help a speech by using numbers to present information. A list of statistics can be boring, but used correctly statistics help an audience understand your point. In the sample speech, several statistics are used to show the cost of the bomb, the damage, etc. Go back and locate several statistics in the speech.

TYPES OF DEVELOPMENT

Comparison and contrast   Comparisons show how things are alike. Contrasts show how things are different. In a way, the whole speech is a comparison between the Manhattan Project and an adventure movie.

Analogy   An analogy compares two things that are different. When the speaker compared the three projects to a "horserace" or a chain reaction to "dominoes," the speaker used an analogy.

Examples   An example is a specific, typical instance of something. The speaker gives examples in the first paragraph. Rather than mentioning a "multi-million dollar movie" and going on to the next point, the speaker gives two specific examples (*Terminator II* and *Aliens III*) to inform the audience what is meant.

Incident   An incident is usually a brief story that makes a point. The response of Enrico Fermi to the possibility of an atomic bomb (it could "make the whole city disappear") is an incident. An incident may be long or short. Often, a lengthy incident becomes too complicated for an audience and must be shortened. Sometimes incidents are created by the speaker to make a point. Hypothetical illustrations should not be presented as the truth, but only as illustrations.

Quotations   When you use the words of another person or of a book or article you have researched, you are using a quotation. As a beginning speaker, you often must give reports on subjects you are just learning about. As a result you usually have to use quotations from authorities to make your points. In the sample speech, the speaker quotes Oppenheimer and Secretary Stimson directly. By using quotations, you can also present facts, opinions, or statistics.

TALK ABOUT IT!   Divide into groups. Take turns reading paragraphs of the sample speech aloud. Discuss the speech's strengths and weaknesses in two to four paragraphs. Use these questions to guide your discussion:

1. Is the speech well organized? Does the introduction get your attention? Is the speaker's purpose clear? Does the conclusion end the speech gracefully?

2. Does the speech present the kind of information suitable to a history class? Is the information interesting?

3. Does the speaker's style get and keep your attention? What kinds of figures of speech does the speaker use?

4. What are the speech's strengths? Weaknesses?

5. Is the speech successful?

ACTIVITY 1   Number a sheet of paper 1-15. Match each of the types of development (numbers 1 through 15) with its name (letters A through H). An item may have more than one answer. If you identify a quotation, for example, make sure you also list it as a fact or opinion or statistic, etc. All the numbered items are from an informative speech on the history of movies in America.

A. Fact   C. Opinion   E. Quotation   G. Analogy
B. Statistic   D. Incident   F. Comparison/contrast H. Example

1. In 1978 the U.S. produced 217 full-length motion pictures.

2. The first movie to win an Academy Award for best picture was *Wings* in 1928.

3. Movies are still the best form of entertainment for young people.

4. The cost of movies has grown tremendously. In 1922, *Robin Hood* cost $1.3 million to make. In 1963, *Cleopatra* cost over $44 million.

5. D. W. Griffith's importance as a director is evident in the film *Nichelodeon*. In this film, a group of inexperienced film makers view Griffith's film *Birth of a Nation*. Coming out of the theater, the group is speechless. They couldn't believe that movies were a form of art.

6. *The Jazz Singer* was the first successful film to include dialogue and music.

7. Local television stations can now choose from over 20,000 feature films.

8. In 1918 the first movies were a magic carpet to wonderful times and places.

9. Back in the 1930s, neighborhood kids could walk to a theater, spend a nickel apiece for a movie ticket, and be treated to two cartoons, an installment of the latest serial, a newsreel, and a full-length motion picture. No wonder a whole generation has fond memories of the movies.

10. "No one," said the newspaper article, "should miss this once-in-a-lifetime motion picture."

11. Movies like *The Ten Commandments*, *Ben-Hur*, and *The Robe* brought many people to theaters in the 1950s.

12. Some movie stars are legends: John Wayne, Marilyn Monroe, Spencer Tracy, Humphrey Bogart, and Mae West are a few.

13. The silent films by Harold Lloyd, Buster Keaton, and Charlie Chaplin are among the best films ever made.

14. During World War II, some directors made films for the government.

15. "In a twelve-month period ending in October, 1983, only twelve films were rated G" (*Time*, June 25, 1984).

SPEAK UP! Prepare a four- to six-minute informative speech. Use the following checklist to be sure you have identified the following: audience, situation, purpose, thesis, types of proof, and types of development used in the speech. Also refer to the evaluation form on pages 112–113.

1. Audience
2. Situation
3. Purpose
4. Thesis
5. Types of Proof
   a. Facts
   b. Opinions
   c. Statistics
6. Types of Development
   a. Comparison/contrast
   b. Analogy
   c. Examples
   d. Incident
   e. Quotations

SUMMARY

A good informative speech uses several types of development. Choosing the right type depends on your audience, subject, and purpose. Together with style, delivery, and organization, the types of development must be adapted to suit the needs of the situation.

Evaluator _____

Informative Speech

Name _____

Instructions: Each category will be rated on a scale of 1–5: 1-poor, 2-fair, 3-good, 4-very good, 5-excellent. Within each category, individual requirements are to be rated with a + or −.

I. <u>SPECIFIC ASSIGNMENT CRITERIA</u>   1 2 3 4 5

_____ Speech met the 4- to 6-minute time limit.

_____ Speech met criteria for an informative speech.

_____ Speech was presented in outline form.

_____ Speech showed evidence of research.

II. <u>ANALYSIS</u>   1 2 3 4 5

_____ Speech adhered to general and specific speech purposes.

_____ Speech was narrow enough to be fully developed and handled adequately in time allotted.

_____ Topic was appropriate for an informative speech.

_____ Topic was appropriate for the audience.

III. <u>SUPPORTING MATERIALS</u>   1 2 3 4 5

_____ Speech utilized sufficient clarifying materials (i.e., examples, illustrations, etc.)

_____ Speech utilized a variety of supporting materials.

_____ Sources were identified where necessary.

_____ Visual aids, if used, were appropriate and used correctly.

IV. <u>INTRODUCTION AND CONCLUSION</u>   1 2 3 4 5

Introduction was properly developed:

_____ Gained audience attention and created interest.

_____ Oriented audience to the speech.

_____ Included a clear and precise thesis statement.

_____ Major ideas were forecast.

Conclusion was developed properly:

_____ Summarized the speech content.

_____ Provided a link back to introductory comments.

_____ Provided an idea for the audience to remember.

V. INTERNAL ORGANIZATION   1 2 3 4 5

_____ Organization of the speech (overall) was clear and easy to follow.

_____ Transitions provided necessary links between ideas.

_____ Speech utilized appropriate signposts and internal summaries.

_____ Organizational pattern was appropriate for topic and type of speech.

VI. DELIVERY TECHNIQUES   1 2 3 4 5

_____ Stance and posture were appropriate.

_____ Eye contact was appropriate.

_____ Facial expressions helped to convey/clarify ideas.

_____ Gestures added emphasis and description.

Vocal delivery was effective:

_____ Appropriate volume   _____ Appropriate rate

_____ Conversational style   _____ Enthusiastic

_____ Clear enunciation   _____ Used pauses correctly

_____ Vocal variety   _____ Fluent delivery

VII. WORD USAGE/LANGUAGE   1 2 3 4 5

_____ Language was direct and made the speaker's point clearly.

_____ Words were used appropriately.

_____ Grammar was appropriate.

_____ Word pronunciations were correct.

_____ Language was suitable for the audience.

COMMENTS AND SUGGESTIONS FOR IMPROVEMENT: TOTAL SCORE _____

14

The Persuasive Speech

Picture This . . .

Week in and week out, you and your friends have been eating lunch in a cafeteria that specializes in bland, boring food. To make matters worse, the people who work in the cafeteria never smile and do not seem to care about what they are doing. The final straw, though, is the announcement that beginning in two weeks, all prices will go up ten percent.

You and your friends decide to take action. It is time for a serious talk with the head dietician and the cafeteria supervisor. In presenting your arguments, you stress the poor quality and lack of variety of the food. You give concrete examples of surly behavior shown by the staff. You conclude by saying that raising the prices is almost criminal and that you and your friends will refuse to pay the higher prices unless conditions change.

The next day you find a new announcement that the prices will go up fifteen percent instead of ten. What might be some possible reasons for your group's failure? Explain.

A. You did not let the head dietician and the cafeteria supervisor know that you understand their problems in running the cafeteria.

B. You did not give reasons why the people who operate and run the cafeteria would benefit from improving the conditions.

C. You did not have proof that most of the people who eat in the cafeteria agree with you.

D. You did not offer constructive suggestions for how conditions could improve.

E. You did not give examples of other cafeterias that offer pleasant service, good meals, and low prices.

INTRODUCTION: The Persuasive Speech

We have all persuaded other people since we first learned to talk. We tried to persuade our parents to let us sleep "just a few more minutes." We tried to convince our brother or sister to share the last cookie in the cookie jar. We tried to persuade a teacher to give a test later in the week, "because everyone else is giving a test on Tuesday."

Everywhere we look or listen, someone is trying to convince us to do something—buy a product, watch a television show, or give money to a charity. We cannot escape persuasion.

Despite our experiences with persuasion, the persuasive speech is one of the most difficult to give. Even when we have good arguments, we sometimes fail to persuade. In this lesson, you will learn what persuasion is and one method of developing a persuasive speech. You will also read a sample persuasive speech for your analysis.

WHAT IS PERSUASION?

When we try to persuade someone, we are trying to *change* the way that person thinks or acts. Because of this, it is often said that persuasion is attitude or behavior change. Attitudes affect much of what we do. For instance, we hold the attitude that stealing is a crime, and so we do not shoplift, even when we do not have enough money to buy what we need. By changing a person's attitudes, we eventually change behavior patterns.

Occasionally persuasion is not meant to change an attitude but to *reinforce* an existing attitude or behavior. People who attend a political rally do not do so because they want to be persuaded to follow the party's platform. They attend because they want to reinforce their beliefs and actions.

On other occasions, persuasion is not designed to change an attitude but is designed to *form a new one*. If we know nothing about the whaling industry, we probably do not have an attitude about how to regulate it to save whales from extinction. A speaker who wants us to contribute money to save the whales would first have to persuade us that there is a problem. Americans are often said to be apathetic on many issues. Often that apathy results from a lack of information. Unless we are informed on a topic, we usually do not have a strong opinion about it.

In some instances you will have a disagreeing audience. It may be impossible to change audience members' attitudes about your topic. Instead you may strive to *modify* their attitudes to be more accepting of yours while maintaining their own.

As a persuader, you must supply sufficient information to achieve your purpose of *changing* an attitude or behavior, *reinforcing* an attitude or behavior, *creating* a new attitude or behavior, or *modifying* an already held attitude or behavior.

ACTIVITY 1   Using examples from your experiences, list a persuasive message you have heard for each of the three persuasive goals.

1. Attitude change:

2. Attitude reinforcement:

3. Attitude creation:

4. Attitude modification:

AN APPROACH TO PERSUASION

Entire books have been written on the process and techniques of persuasion. However, there is one persuasive process that is especially suitable for the persuasive speech. Known as the Motivated Sequence, it was developed by two college speech professors, Alan Monroe and Douglas Ehninger. The Motivated Sequence has five steps. You will learn the logic behind each and will read a speech that incorporates all five.

The Motivated Sequence

According to Alan Monroe and Douglas Ehninger, the five steps in the persuasive process are:

1. Attention step
2. Need step
3. Satisfaction step
4. Visualization step
5. Action step

The basic idea behind these five steps is that you must give your listener a *reason* to change an idea or behavior or to adopt a new one. In other words, you must motivate that person.

How do you motivate someone? Think about yourself. What motivates you to clean a room, start an exercise program, or drive more carefully? In some instances, it is fear. A finicky friend may be coming to visit, your doctor warned you about excess weight, or you may have had a near accident on the highway. You can also be motivated by positive rewards. You enjoy making your surroundings pretty, you may fit into the new jeans you just bought, or your insurance rates will go down because of your good driving record.

Whether we are motivated through positive or negative means, the Motivated Sequence provides an organized system for approaching persuasion. Consider the logic of each step.

Attention step

The first step in the sequence is getting the listener's attention. It is important to capture the audience's interest immediately, because you will never achieve your goal unless the audience wants to hear more.

Need step

This is one of the most important steps in the Motivated Sequence. In this step, you give the listener a reason or a set of reasons to accept your message. The need usually takes the form of one or more problems. Presenting problems alone will not guarantee a successful need step; the listeners must identify with the problems. In some way, listeners must feel a personal involvement.

According to Abraham Maslow, there are five basic human needs. By using these five needs as the basis for the need step, you are better able to involve the audience. Maslow identifies the five needs as:

1. Physiological   4. Self-esteem
2. Safety   5. Self-actualization
3. Belongingness

Physiological needs refer to these things that help keep us alive—food, water, and shelter are the most common. Television advertising often appeals to these needs. Think of the number of commercials you have seen for food; many address nutritional needs as well as satisfaction of hunger.

Safety needs involve our sense of security. Advertising for smoke detectors, insurance, or car batteries often appeal to this need.

Belongingness involves our wanting to have friends or to be loved by others. No one can live alone. We need human contact to live healthy lives. We need to be accepted by others. Advertising, which suggests we will be surrounded by friends or attractive members of the opposite sex by using a certain product, appeals to this need. Watch commercials for toothpaste, mouthwash, or soap and determine if they appeal to our need for affection from others.

Self-esteem refers to our feelings about ourselves. We need to like ourselves to be well-adjusted individuals. Many public service announcements appeal to this need. For instance, advertising that encourages people to donate money to a charity is intended to make us feel good about what we have done. We get a sense that we are "good people" for helping others.

Self-actualization, the final need, means that we realize all our potential. The U.S. Army appeal—"Be all that you can be in the Army"—is a self-actualization appeal.

Determine if the audience members will feel a threat to any of these five needs in Maslow's pyramid if the problem you present is not solved.

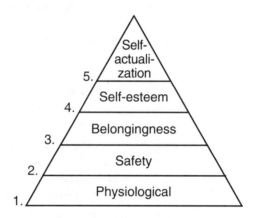

ACTIVITY 2   Using examples from magazines and newspapers, identify products that incorporate one of the five needs. Locate at least two examples for each need and write an explanation for your choices.

1. Physiological:

2. Safety:

3. Belongingness:

4. Self-esteem:

5. Self-actualization:

Satisfaction step   After presenting a need, it is important to tell audience members how to eliminate or reduce that need. This is done through the satisfaction or solution step. In this step, you clearly identify the attitude or behavior you want to change. In most advertising it is a simple message: "Buy our product." In a speech it usually involves suggesting a plan of action or alternative behaviors, such as exercising fifteen minutes a day.

Visualization step   This step helps listeners understand how the solution works. If you are trying to convince someone to buy a personal computer, the visualization step would explain everything that the computer can do. You would be able to help your listener picture using it for writing reports or balancing the family budget. In this step, you explain how the solution actually eliminates the need. This is an important step because an audience should be convinced that the solution actually satisfies the need.

Action step   The final step informs listeners how to implement the solution. If you were trying to persuade everyone to write to a member of Congress in favor of a certain bill, you would give specific information about the senator or representative. You would give the names and addresses, and how to best write the letter.

The action step provides a way for the audience to carry through with the solution. It makes it appear that the audience can influence the needs. Unless listeners believe they personally can do something, you are less likely to change their attitudes.

A SAMPLE PERSUASIVE SPEECH

A persuasive speech is the most difficult type to give because there are two sides to every issue. Not everyone in the audience will agree with your position. If all audience members did agree with you, there would be little reason to persuade. The following speech is an example of a topic for which there are two sides. As you read the speech notice how the Motivated Sequence is used to change attitudes. Each step is indicated in the margin.

WINNING ISN'T EVERYTHING

Attention Step

Lance Sprague loved football. He wanted to be just like the professional players whose posters decorated his room. But Lance's fumbled punt cost his team the league championship. After that, Lance's teammates ignored him. The coach yelled at him. Though his best friend tried to soothe his feelings, his brother said he couldn't believe that Lance was such a klutz. The day after the game, Lance quit football and never played or watched it again.

Lance's reaction to what he perceived as failure is more extreme than most of ours, but most of us have probably felt like athletic failures at one time or another. Perhaps you were the last one chosen in grade school every time you divided into softball teams. Or perhaps you never made it on the varsity team. Or perhaps you had to have a job after school and could never become a "football hero."

Even if you are a successful athlete, you probably feel other types of pressure. There aren't enough hours in the day to train properly, do your assignments for class, and still have time for friends and family.

Whichever of these feelings relate to you, they all highlight some of the problems we have today because of a strong emphasis on sports in many schools.

Need Step

Schools are supposed to be for education of the mind first. In 1983 a study of U.S. schools, *A Nation at Risk*, alerted us that our schools and students were falling behind our competitors'. Ten years later, studies continued to show declining test scores, high drop-out rates, and students graduating without some of the basic skills for the work force. Our limited resources for education need to maximize learning. Yet emphasis on competitive sports can detract from learning in many ways.

This is not to say that sports have no value in our schools. They teach self-discipline and prepare students for a competitive world. However, sports programs need to be put in perspective. Sports should be a part of school programs but should not dominate them.

Currently sports tend to dominate some school scheduling. Long practices, frequent pep rallies, and the games themselves—including travel time—all disrupt school and study schedules. Too often participation in sports takes students and teachers out of classes.

According to Paul Fink, the personnel director in a suburban school district, teachers are sometimes hired because they can coach, not because they are the best teachers. And sometimes teachers with little or no knowledge of a sport are forced to coach because the school must have a team in every sport.

Coaches are under pressure to win. And some push students so hard that school and family life are sacrificed. The quest for a championship has created a "star system" whereby the most athletically talented students monopolize coaching time. Students who ride the bench or don't make the team feel like failures.

But even the stars don't always win. Countless star athletes cannot qualify for athletic scholarships because their grades are not good enough. Even students who can maintain their grades often push themselves because they have visions of being pro heroes. However, only a small percentage of high school athletes make it in college, and only one in tens of thousands will fulfill the dream of being a professional.

Students who are more realistic about the future can also be victimized by the system. Sports-related injuries cannot be ignored. Each year many students are injured in sports to the extent of needing a doctor's care. Twelve million students will suffer permanent physical injury before reaching the age of 18. Seventy-five percent of orthopedists surveyed in a major medical publication recommended a deemphasis on sports in schools.

While "stars" are competing, being injured, and perhaps being burned out because of the pressures from coaches, fans, and parents, they and other students are not receiving the physical education needed to be physically fit. Emphasis on competitive team sports means students may not be taught sports they can enjoy after they leave school such as swimming, tennis, volleyball, or softball. According to a report in *Education USA* the physical fitness of the average American student, which rose slightly under President Kennedy's physical fitness program in the early 1960s, stabilized from 1965 to 1975 and thereafter declined. Given the increased emphasis on sports and addition of girls' sports during that same period, this fact is even more shocking.

Satisfaction Step   Solving these problems should not be impossible. The *Nation at Risk* and its responses clearly show motivation for change exists. People who are concerned about education in our country are calling for a change in priorities—from football to physics, from higher scores on the field to higher scores on the reading tests.

Visualization Step   A number of specific changes are attractive. Infringements on class time must be strictly limited. State eligibility requirements for student athletes must be raised. It is not too much to expect a student to pass all of his or her classes before being allowed to participate in sports.

At the junior high level and lower, competitive sports must be deemphasized in favor of intramurals. Equal access to facilities, random selection of teams, and regular faculty-student playtime are all worthy innovations.

Cooperation with parent-volunteers and community programs can ensure that competitive outlets are available for students whose parents want supervised competitive programs. But the schools must refocus their attention on academics by putting the "extra" back in extracurricular.

Action Step

The *Nation at Risk* got the ball rolling toward educational reform. Let's pass it along to those who can make a difference. You must be part of the solution. Talk to school principals or school board members. Write to your state legislator who will be considering several bills to upgrade eligibility requirements.

We cannot afford more victims of overemphasis on winning and competing. Our schools should make students feel like winners—whether they win on the field or in the classroom. And more important, our schools should prepare students to be winners after they leave school.

TALK ABOUT IT!

Working in groups of four or five people, analyze the persuasive speech. Find examples of appeals to the human needs Maslow identified. What type of introduction was used? What is the organizational pattern? Outline the speech and identify transitional statements. Who is the audience for the speech? How can you tell? How would your group improve the speech? Be specific in your suggestions.

ACTIVITY 3

Assume you are presenting the opposing viewpoint—sports should receive more attention in the schools. Which of Maslow's needs would your speech appeal to? Explain your answer in one or two paragraphs.

EVALUATING THE PERSUASIVE SPEECH

A persuasive speech can be evaluated by measuring attitude change or by identifying behavioral changes. It is often helpful to ask people for their opinions on the speech topic before you give the speech. After its conclusion, survey the audience again to determine if there were attitude changes.

SPEAK UP!

Prepare a five- to seven-minute speech to persuade. Use the steps in the Motivated Sequence, as well as the evaluation form at the end of this lesson to guide your preparation. Select a topic you feel strongly about. Use research to support your point of view. Prepare an opinion scale and distribute it to your audience before you give the speech. Distribute a second scale after the speech. Did your speech change attitudes?

SUMMARY

Persuasive speeches are the most difficult to give because they aim at changing people's attitudes and behaviors. In preparing a persuasive message, you must keep the audience's needs in mind. Your listeners must feel they are affected by the problems you describe, and they must feel they can be a part of the solution.

Create a motivation for change by appealing to one of the five needs identified by Maslow: physiological, safety, belongingness, self-esteem, or self-actualization.

Use the Motivated Sequence to assist in organizing your arguments. The Motivated Sequence requires that you gain the audience's attention, establish a need for change, provide a means of satisfying the need, visualize the solution, and describe how the audience can act on the solution.

Evaluator _____

Persuasive Speech

Name _____

Instructions: Each category will be rated on a scale of 1–5: 1-poor, 2-fair, 3-good, 4-very good, 5-excellent. Within each category, individual requirements are to be rated with a + or −.

I. <u>SPECIFIC ASSIGNMENT CRITERIA</u>   1 2 3 4 5

    _____ Speech met the 5- to 7-minute time limit.

    _____ Speech was persuasive in nature.

    _____ Speech was presented in outline form.

    _____ Speech showed evidence of research.

II. <u>ANALYSIS</u>   1 2 3 4 5

    _____ Speech adhered to general and specific speech purposes.

    _____ Speech was narrow enough to be fully developed and handled adequately in time allotted.

    _____ Topic was appropriate for persuasive speech.

    _____ Established a need for the audience to listen.

III. <u>SUPPORTING MATERIALS</u>   1 2 3 4 5

    _____ Speech utilized sufficient clarifying materials (i.e., examples, illustrations, etc.)

    _____ Speech utilized a variety of supporting materials.

    _____ Sources were identified where necessary.

    _____ Visual aids, if used, were appropriate and used correctly.

IV. <u>INTRODUCTION AND CONCLUSION</u>   1 2 3 4 5

Introduction was properly developed:

    _____ Gained audience attention and created interest.

    _____ Oriented audience to the speech.

    _____ Included a clear and precise thesis statement.

    _____ Major ideas were forecast.

Conclusion was developed:

    _____ Summarized the speech content.

    _____ Provided a link back to introductory comments.

    _____ Provided an idea for the audience to remember.

V. INTERNAL ORGANIZATION
1 2 3 4 5

_____ Organization of the speech (overall) was clear and easy to follow.

_____ Transitions provided necessary links between ideas.

_____ Speech utilized appropriate transitions and internal summaries.

_____ Followed steps in the Motivated Sequence.

VI. DELIVERY TECHNIQUES
1 2 3 4 5

_____ Stance and posture were appropriate.

_____ Eye contact was appropriate.

_____ Facial expressions helped to convey/clarify ideas.

_____ Gestures added emphasis and description.

Vocal delivery was effective:

_____ Appropriate volume	_____ Appropriate rate
_____ Conversational style	_____ Enthusiastic
_____ Clear enunciation	_____ Used pauses correctly
_____ Vocal variety	_____ Fluent

VII. PERSUASIVE STRATEGIES
1 2 3 4 5

_____ Supported arguments with credible sources.

_____ Provided a satisfaction step.

_____ Provided a visualization step.

_____ Provided an action step.

_____ Used appropriate persuasive strategies (e.g., one-sided or two-sided arguments, fear appeals, logical appeals, etc.).

VIII. WORD USAGE/LANGUAGE
1 2 3 4 5

_____ Language was direct and made the speaker's point clearly.

_____ Words were used appropriately.

_____ Grammar was appropriate.

_____ Word pronunciations were correct.

_____ Language was suitable for the audience.

COMMENTS AND SUGGESTIONS FOR IMPROVEMENT: TOTAL SCORE _____

GLOSSARY

Abstract Lacking preciseness. Words that create general rather than specific mental pictures.

Analogy A way of comparing two things that are different.

Antithesis The use of parallel structure, with the exception that opposites must be paired together.

Articulation The act or manner of expressing sounds readily, clearly, and effectively with one's voice.

Attributing Identifying in a speech or in a bibliography the source of a quotation, an idea, or a piece of information.

Audience Analysis The process a speaker uses to determine the interests, needs, knowledge level, attitudes, and demographics of an audience as they relate to the speaker's purpose.

Cause-Effect An organizational pattern in which the first part of the speech describes the causes or reasons for a problem and the second part spells out the effects or results of the problem.

Chronological An organizational pattern which uses time sequence as a framework.

Clarity The quality or state of being understandable through proper pronunciation and articulation, or the ability to state ideas in a clear, understandable manner.

Classification An organizational pattern which places ideas into categories or classes as a framework.

Conclusion The part of speech which summarizes the major ideas. It is given at the end of the speech.

Credibility The ability of a speaker to be believed by an audience.

Critical Listening Listening to a speaker with a questioning, evaluative frame of reference.

Demographic Of or relating to the study of human populations especially with reference to size, distribution, and vital statistics. In public speaking, an analysis of age, gender, occupation, educational background, religion, political background, and ethnic or cultural background of an audience.

Demonstration Speech A speech which explains how to do something by actually showing an audience how.

Economy Stating ideas as briefly as possible without sacrificing clarity or grace.

Enunciation The act or manner of forming vocal sounds clearly and distinctly.

Evaluation The process of examining and judging a speech in terms of specific criteria.

Exaggeration The overstatement of an idea to emphasize a point.

External Transition A means of connecting points between different sections of a speech.

Eye Contact A speaker's communication with an audience that involves looking directly into the eyes of audience members.

Feedback Verbal and nonverbal responses to a speech by the audience. Feedback allows a speaker to check on whether a result is being achieved.

Framing Pausing slightly before and after a word or phrase to give it emphasis.

Gender The sex of the audience member—male or female.

Gestures The use of motions of the body, especially the arms and hands as a means of expression.

Hidden Agenda A purpose which is intentionally unstated or concealed behind another purpose.

Impromptu Delivery A type of delivery which is not rehearsed and does not involve notes or prior planning.

Internal Transition A means of relating information within a section of a speech.

Introduction The part of a speech which prepares an audience for what is to be presented in the body.

Irony The use of a particular word with the intention of conveying the opposite of its normal meaning.

Jargon Language made up of specialized, technical words of a specific job, hobby, or social group.

Manuscript Delivery A type of delivery in which the speaker uses a manuscript for a speech.

Memorized Delivery A type of delivery in which the speaker has committed a speech to memory.

Metaphor A figure of speech containing a direct comparison without using the words like or *as* such as "Her words were drops of acid."

Motivated Sequence A persuasive process involving five steps: attention, need, satisfaction, visualization, and action.

Narrowing The process of developing a specific speech topic to fit the purpose of the speech, the audience, the occasion, and the time requirements.

Nonverbal Communication using means, such as gestures, other than spoken or written language.

Occasion Analysis The process a speaker uses to determine how the setting, circumstances, and events surrounding a speech will affect topic selection, delivery, and length of the speech.

Outline Delivery A type of delivery of a speech which uses an outline or key words and phrases on paper to serve as reminders to the speaker.

Parallel Structure Stating ideas that are logically related in a similar way.

Persuade To change attitudes or behaviors of audience members.

Pitch The degree of highness or lowness in a speaker's voice.

Posture The position or bearing of the body.

Problem-Solution An organizational pattern of a speech in which the first part of the speech spells out a problem and the second part gives an answer or solution to the problem.

Purpose Statement A formal declaration by the speaker to him or herself and to the audience regarding what will be accomplished in the speech.

Rate In public speaking, the speed at which one talks.

Repetition The repeating of a word, phrase, idea, or sound.

Rhetorical Question A question designed to produce an effect and not to draw an answer from the audience.

Simile A comparison between two unlike things with the use of the words *like* or *as*.

Situation All the factors surrounding a speech—location, time, audience composition, and audience's reason for attending.

Slang Informal, nonstandard language, often unique to a group.

Spatial An organizational pattern of a speech which uses physical space as a framework; often used in informative speeches and sometimes in entertainment speeches.

Speech Purpose The reason for a speech, or what the speaker is trying to accomplish. For example, informing, persuading, and entertaining are all speech purposes.

Speech to Entertain A speech which tries to gain and keep the audience's attention and create a pleasant diversion.

Speech to Inform A speech which tries to provide an audience new information about a specific topic.

Speech to Persuade A speech which is intended to change the attitudes or behavior of audience members.

Stagefright Nervousness felt as a result of giving a speech.

Startling Statement A statement used in a speech, usually in the introduction, to get the audience's attention quickly by making the audience think of something in a way not considered before.

Style The way something is said or done.

Subordination The process of dividing material into more specific information. For example, into major points, then subpoints under the major points, and then into examples under the subpoint, and so on.

Supportive Materials Information which serves to defend or prove the point being made by a speaker. For example, quotations from experts, facts, and statistics are all types of supporting materials.

Thesis Statement The speaker's point of view on his or her subject stated in a single sentence.

Tone A particular quality or way of sounding that expresses some meaning, feeling, or attitude.

Trite Words or statements made commonplace by constant use or repetition.

Understatement The act of saying less than one really means in order to emphasize a point.

Visual Aid An instructional device, such as a chalkboard, poster, or movie that appeals chiefly to vision.

Volume The degree of loudness and softness in a speaker's voice.

INDEX